Language across the Curriculum in the Elementary Grades

Language across the Curriculum in the Elementary Grades

Christopher Thaiss
George Mason University

ERIC Clearinghouse on Reading and Communication Skills
Office of Educational Research and Improvement
U.S. Department of Education

National Council of Teachers of English
1111 Kenyon Road, Urbana, Illinois 61801

Consultant Readers: Angela M. Jaggar, Sister Rosemary Winkeljohann

Staff Editor: Jane M. Curran

Book Design: Tom Kovacs for TGK Design

NCTE Stock Number 25735

Published 1986 by the ERIC Clearinghouse on Reading and Communication Skills and the National Council of Teachers of English, 1111 Kenyon Road, Urbana, Illinois 61801

This publication was prepared with funding from the Office of Educational Research and Improvement, U.S. Department of Education, under Contract No. 400-83-0025. Contractors undertaking such projects under government sponsorship are encouraged to express freely their judgment in professional and technical matters. Prior to publication, the manuscript was submitted to the National Council of Teachers of English for critical review and determination of professional competence. This publication has met such standards. Points of view or opinions, however, do not necessarily represent the official view or opinions of either the National Council of Teachers of English or the Office of Educational Research and Improvement.

Library of Congress Cataloging-in-Publication Data
Thaiss, Christopher J., 1948–
    Language across the curriculum in the elementary grades.

    Includes bibliographies.
    1. Language arts (Elementary)—United States.
2. Language arts—United States—Correlation with
content subjects.   I. ERIC Clearinghouse on Reading
and Communication Skills.   II. National Council of
Teachers of English.   III. Title.
LB1576.T483 1986   372.6'043   86-2447
ISBN 0-8141-2573-5

Contents

Acknowledgments

It would be impossible for me to acknowledge all those who, through their conversation, through their writing, or through the example of their teaching, have helped me to become capable enough and learned enough to produce this book. It must suffice that I pay some of this debt in the text itself, through my citations of some of the writers who have influenced and inspired me. How wonderful to realize that we who share the love of language and learning can build a community through our gifts of writing.

Let me thank somewhat more explicitly, but still wholly inadequately, my colleagues at George Mason University, in the English Department and in the Plan for Alternative General Education, who each day show countless examples of concern for students and intellectual commitment to teaching. Let me particularly thank Elizabeth Hedley, Executive Assistant of the Plan for Alternative General Education, who continually demonstrates that the excellent teacher need not be defined by the classroom.

My thanks also go to Charles Suhor, Deputy Executive Director of the National Council of Teachers of English and Director of the ERIC Clearinghouse on Reading and Communication Skills, who conceived of this project and invited me to take it on. Thanks also to Paul O'Dea, NCTE Coordinator of Publications, and Jane Christensen, NCTE Associate Executive Director, for their enthusiasm and support.

This book could not have come into being without the landmark contributions to theory and practice by the National Writing Project, whose teacher/consultants provide one of the best examples of networking in the world today. Whatever I have acquired of appreciation for the work of the elementary teacher has come to me through the talk and writing I have shared, since 1978, with the members of the Northern Virginia site of the NWP. Special thanks are due my friend and colleague Don Gallehr, director of the Northern Virginia project, whose style—of leadership and of composition—shapes the project, and whose advice I relied on in identifying the teachers who might serve as the focuses of this study.

The most obvious debt I owe is to the teachers whose thoughts, words, and deeds are displayed here. One could not ask for more gracious and enthusiastic collaborators than Cynthia Dietz, Carin Hauser, Al Lengel, Mary Browning Schulman, and Elly Uehling. Nor could one ask for more gracious hosts than the students, from six to twelve years old, who made me feel at home in their classrooms by treating me as one of the gang. Working among people like these, who would not want to write and teach?

Those for whom all thanks are inadequate, but who appreciate me far beyond all deserving, are my sons, Jeff, Jimmy, Christopher, and Flannery, who always teach the essential subjects and who never bore.

I owe the most, for this and for everything else of meaning to me, to my children's true mentor, Ann Jeffries-Thaiss, who teaches with the purest brilliance and grace I will ever know. Her school I would not want to miss for even one day.

Finally, I wish to acknowledge my debt to one member of the community of lovers of language and learning: the late John Holt, whose courage and wisdom live on in his books and in the deeds of the thousands of teachers and parents he has inspired. I dedicate this work to his memory.

C. J. T.
George Mason University
October 1985

Foreword

The Educational Resources Information Center (ERIC) is a national information system operated by the Office of Educational Research and Improvement (OERI) of the U.S. Department of Education. It provides ready access to descriptions of exemplary programs, research and development efforts, and related information useful in developing effective educational programs.

Through its network of specialized centers or clearinghouses, each of which is responsible for a particular educational area, ERIC acquires, evaluates, abstracts, and indexes current significant information and lists this information in its reference publications.

ERIC/RCS, the ERIC Clearinghouse on Reading and Communication Skills, disseminates educational information related to research, instruction, and professional preparation at all levels and in all institutions. The scope of interest of the Clearinghouse includes relevant research reports, literature reviews, curriculum guides and descriptions, conference papers, project or program reviews, and other print materials related to reading, English, educational journalism, and speech communication.

The ERIC system has already made available—through the ERIC Document Reproduction System—much informative data. However, if the findings of specific educational research are to be intelligible to teachers and applicable to teaching, considerable amounts of data must be reevaluated, focused, and translated into a different context. Rather than resting at the point of making research reports readily accessible, OERI has directed the clearinghouses to work with professional organizations in developing information analysis papers in specific areas within the scope of the clearinghouses.

ERIC is pleased to cooperate with the National Council of Teachers of English in making *Language across the Curriculum in the Elementary Grades* available.

Charles Suhor
Director, ERIC/RCS

1 The Mind and the Word

Anyone who writes about learning has to admit that nobody can prove that one method of teaching categorically surpasses another. We all know that learning, for each of us, takes place all the time; the world is coming to us constantly, and our minds, through our bodies and through our conscious processes, are constantly assimilating bits and pieces of that world and shaping them into patterns of ideas and expectations. We are more full of receptors than we can possibly be aware: indeed, an incredible amount of our knowledge comes to us unconsciously. Furthermore, the learning process is so subtle and often so nearly imperceptible that even theories of genetically trans-ferred knowledge continue to flourish despite the efforts of the social and behavioral sciences to assert the cultural, environmental basis of learning. The rise of cognitive science, which has given us such in-valuable metaphors as *right-brain* and *left-brain* thinking, represents nothing so much as our recognition of the mystery of learning.

Of course, once we acknowledge the mystery of learning, the more open we should become to new and varied ways of teaching. Even more important, we should become more fascinated observers of our children as they learn—we should become students of our students. Perhaps the most compelling feature of the best writing about chil-dren's learning of language over the past few decades has been its fascinated focus on the child. From Piaget to Donaldson to Graves, these writers give us the great pleasure—adventure, really—of hearing how young minds explore the world and shape it, make sense of it, through what they say and write. Who can resist, for example, the wonder in a writer such as John Holt (1967) as he reports in his diary the discoveries of twenty-five-month-old Lisa?

> Later, Lisa walked round and round the balloon, singing, more or less, her own version of "Ring-around-a-rosie." As she sang it, she began to change it, until before long it had become an entirely different song. Much of what she says, sings, and does, is like this; it starts out as one thing, and gradually turns into another. A musician might call it variations on a theme. (5)

We come to know real people through this research, and this is prob-ably its most important lesson. Rather than comparing educational

1

"treatments" and attempting to measure "results" through numerical comparisons, these scholars look at many individuals, observing each child closely and trying to build, as might a poet, as full an understanding as possible of what is happening in the child and in the world the child affects. These writers take a very optimistic view of children. They trust them, as James Britton said all teachers must, to show us parents, teachers, and researchers how to teach and how to observe. For those of us who must daily attempt to mediate between our students and the mandated curricula of schools and school boards, this open-minded attention to the children, this research attitude, would also seem the best, maybe the only, way of letting us know what to teach and when.

You might wonder why I've begun this little book on *language across the curriculum* with this brief exclamation on attitudes and research methods. I've started this way because my practice, my reflection, and my talk with other teachers and parents on this phenomenon have led me to realize that language across the curriculum is not primarily a teaching method or a set of activities, but is basically a way to describe fundamental principles that some teachers bring to, and have learned from, their calling. Beyond this, language across the curriculum also describes how all of us—at any age—do a great deal of our learning. Language across the curriculum can be nurtured or hindered through methods and activities, but even the soundest of methods will be hollow and inflexible if the teacher doesn't believe in and actively understand this way of thinking about learning. It is not a coincidence that the teachers and researchers who have written most compellingly about language across the curriculum have "discovered" it, as it were, after countless hours of watching, listening to, and talking with children. They have discovered that language across the curriculum is something that happens continuously in classrooms and in homes and on playgrounds, whether we wish it to or not, and that much learning—when we really mean learning, not just clock-watching—can't happen without it. It may be possible, of course, to learn without language, if by language we mean only words and other symbols; after all, we recognize faces, imitate actions, and form a multitude of other impressions without the tools of language. Nevertheless, when we speak of *curriculum,* we mean almost exclusively a reality that is presented to us through words and symbols, either written or spoken. And in this context, researcher after researcher has found that to own, to know, anything of the world requires the child's manipulation of it through words and symbols. It follows from this that to encourage language across the curriculum, methods and activities would include *anything* students do and teachers design that brings into the learning process as much language use—talking, writing, listening, reading—as possible. The concept requires further that teachers exploit imaginatively, as occasions for learning, anything that children want to talk and write about.

Given this definition, a language-across-the-curriculum attitude implies the restructuring of curricula away from so-called "coverage" of content and toward creation of opportunities for such means of learning as discussions, games, and in-class writing projects. Since conversation and composing will invariably spark a group to new ideas and unpredicted curiosity, this definition also implies the willingness of adults (e.g., teachers and principals) to let the learning move as it may, at least within broad limits.

Chapter two will "flesh out" the theory of language across the curriculum through a summary and analysis of the landmark research in this field over the last two decades. It will also touch on the major disciplines in order to cite significant research and to suggest practical techniques for bringing a learning-through-language approach to bear on the teaching of all subjects.

The largest portion of this small book, chapters three through seven, will take you into five classrooms and introduce you to five teachers whose nurturing of learning through language, in every subject area, shows the imagination and commitment I've described. You will meet these teachers not only through my narratives but also through their own words, as they describe further details of their practice and how that practice has been shaped by theory and experience. I've chosen these five for various reasons. First, all are recognized in their schools and in their region as excellent teachers, professionals who have studied principles of classroom research and have written about the learners they lead. Second, their students represent grades one through six, thus providing the reader with numerous examples of how language across the curriculum occurs among children of widely varying interests and levels of sophistication. Third, these teachers work in different types of classes and with students to whom the system gives distinctive, often isolating, labels: learning disabled, speech impaired, gifted and talented, and, of course, "regular." These differing situations show how language across the curriculum can cut across and often blur—in a positive way—these distinctions. Finally, I chose these teachers because the richness of their work makes it easy for me as the observer to describe scenes and projects on which fellow teachers can exert their own imaginative analysis.

Reference

Holt, John. *How Children Learn*. New York: Dell, 1967. Rev. ed., 1983.

2 Making Every Subject Language Rich

Language across the curriculum is still an unwieldy term for many people in education. It is common, for example, for workshops in language across the curriculum to be misunderstood as concerning its subtheme *writing across the curriculum,* itself an exciting, burgeoning concept, but far less encompassing. Writing across the curriculum will be a major concern in this survey of theory and practice and in the classroom vignettes to follow, but we need to distinguish it from the larger idea for an important reason. Writing is usually thought of as being done by elementary-age children more frequently *in* school than out, or *for* school rather than for other purposes. Though this generalization may not be entirely true, most would agree that writing in the school is usually initiated by the teacher. Hence, like most other elements of the curriculum, writing is thought of as something "we" would like "them" to do and know, because they'll need to know how to write for their future schooling and beyond. As a result, books and articles on writing across the curriculum tend to focus on describing assignments and management techniques that will make writing exciting to the students. Of course, many have argued that writing is just as natural a mode of language as is talking or listening, and that it is the schools' limited, mechanical view of writing that has made students resist it (a topic to be discussed later in the chapter). Nevertheless, we tend to view writing as one more subject that we teach to students.

By contrast, *language* across the curriculum, since it includes talking and listening, describes both naturally occurring phenomena (natural in the sense that most children talk and listen from infancy) and formal goals and activities in the school. The irony of talk in schools is that probably more ink has been spilled and more arguments in the teachers' lounge have been generated over how to quell talk than how to encourage it. Talk within the group, because of its tendency to move associatively—to take off on tangents—has often been seen as the enemy of curriculum, particularly in areas where teachers feel pressured to accomplish "coverage" objectives or to move from topic to topic, skill to skill, according to a fixed plan. As long as

4

teachers and administrators do not acknowledge the vital role of all the language modes in their students' learning, they will not be likely to make room in their curricula for the volatility and unpredictability of talk.

Learning through Language

Consequently, reports of research findings on the mesh between language and learning have been aimed at convincing school leaders of the vital need for active expression by all children in all school subjects. Central to this movement have been the books by James Britton, Douglas Barnes, and their associates in the British Schools Council Project, a research project ongoing since the 1960s. In *Language and Learning* (1970), Britton reported his original research with children from infancy through adolescence and drew on findings of Jean Piaget, Edward Sapir, Jerome Bruner, Suzanne Langer, and many others. He concluded that from infancy onward the most important function of talk, as of writing, is "commentary" (making sense for oneself out of the randomness of perceptions) and that we must speak or write about an experience in order to understand it and thus to be able to use it to create expectations. While noting, with the Russian linguist Lev Vygotsky (1962), that much of the private talking aloud that goes on in early childhood becomes "inner speech" later on, Britton nevertheless demonstrates that older children and adults turn to verbalizing in times of stress and confusion (as we say, "just to get our thinking straight" or to "talk it out"). Putting our thoughts into words, wrote Vygotsky, is our only means of selecting among the myriad images that assault our minds, and our only way of giving them a form that we can deal with. Extending this idea, Julian Jaynes (1977) argued that consciousness is not possible without verbalization, either internal or aloud, because words are our only means of bringing the new, the unknown, into the world with which we are familiar. Moreover, as Janet Emig (1977), William Irmscher (1979), and many others have said, we can only assimilate new information through "our own" words; i.e., words with which we are comfortable, whose meanings we feel we can control. Thus, we can't understand another person's ideas merely by reading and trying to remember his or her words.

We can illustrate this by considering any conversation in which one person is trying to explain something to another. Inevitably, the explainer must repeat parts of the explanation in response to questions from the listener. Usually this repetition involves revising the message to add details or to change the vocabulary. Ironically, but not surprisingly, this give-and-take frequently leads the explainer to realize that he or she may not really have understood what he or she is trying to explain to the other person.

We might say that this typical process reveals a flaw in communication, but language researchers would say that this mutual groping for clarity is part of the very nature and function of language. Written or spoken, they would say, language is first and foremost our best tool for trying to understand; only secondarily is it a tool for communication. Moreover, they say, neither function is efficient; when we try to speak or write to others, we are betting (hoping) that our audience will give the same "sense" to our words that we do. But this is unlikely, since each person attaches idiosyncratic, unshared meanings to many words. Because these personal meanings are themselves changed over time, our words tend to lose their ability to communicate, even with ourselves. Thus, we rarely reuse the same words and sentences to explain what we think is the same idea or to recall an event for a second time. The difficulty is compounded when we try to relate these ideas and events to someone else. As Linda Flower (1979) has shown, most of our apparent effort to communicate with others is actually our further effort to make meaning for ourselves. Invariably, we fall short.

This theory of language and learning, insofar as it is true, has immense consequences for the classroom, no matter what subject is being studied. I will discuss three consequences in detail.

1. *Children will understand, and thus remember, only what they have the opportunity to talk about (and, perhaps, to write about, sing about, draw, make plays about, etc.).*

Jerome Bruner (1966), Janet Emig (1971, 1983), and Nancy Martin et al. (1976) are among those whose research emphasizes this first consequence. Martin and her colleagues present transcriptions of student dialogues in science labs, which show how such talk causes each person to raise new questions about an experiment and to allow the students to help one another understand the observations. Anne Wotring and Robert Tierney (1981) show similar results in relation to journals kept by high school biology and chemistry students, while Barry Beyer (1980) and especially Donald Holsinger (1983) show how a variety of language activities is essential to any understanding of history. Barbara King (1982) and Minja Paik and Eugene Norris (1983) are among those who write of this phenomenon in mathematics. Specific classroom practices that derive from this consequence are described in the chapters that follow. Other sources of language-to-learn activities across the curriculum at the elementary and preschool levels are Stephen Tchudi and Susan Tchudi (1983) and Ann Jeffries-Thaiss and the author (1984).

Crucial to understanding all these writers' work is James Britton's concept of the *spectator* versus the *participant*. Most of our language use is in the spectator role, in which we give order to an experience and try to express our feelings about it. Less frequent, except in traditional school assignments, is participant language, with which we try to "get things done" between us and others. Developmentally, giving the spectator every occasion to play with ideas and try out interpretations is crucial if the participant is ever to emerge. Those school programs that encourage students to write and speak mainly in the participant mode (through recitations, oral reports, and written tests) are not really language-across-the-curriculum programs; they are depending on someone else—the parents and the children themselves—to do the important, basic work. In such programs, the few who are already well educated in the spectator role will succeed as participants, while most will do mediocre or poor work.

Where learning, i.e., language, is really important in a curriculum, the roles of both spectator and participant will be played, with the spectator receiving top billing. The child will still give oral presentations and write reports and stories, but more time and effort will be devoted to less formal activities—such as discussions, games, journal writing—that both promote the spectator's understanding of perceptions and ideas, and help children become relaxed, confident language users. In what I call the language-rich, learning-intensive classroom, a spirit of experimentation, of play (which, as John Holt reminds us, is serious business for children), will reign. The teacher will be more a listener than a talker, and most of his or her talk will be in response to the children, either as questioner, to help the children take their thinking in new directions, or as *one* source (not *the* source) of information. Writing will contribute to this experimental spirit through emphasis on its great value as a tool of discovery and as a tool of imagination. As the following chapters will show, corroborating the findings of Donald Graves (1983), Lucy McCormick Calkins (1983), and others, young children find writing, like drawing, to be a comfortable way of giving form to their ideas and of claiming ownership of what they know. Nothing is quite like the pride children feel in the stories they write, whether fantasy or nonfiction.

Furthermore, children's writing, like their talk, gives them and others—including the teacher—further food for thought. Emig (1977) and Donald Murray (1983, 1985) have written with particular power of writing's ability to take us to insights, to new ways of understanding. When writing for ourselves in journal format or in freewriting exercises (see Ken Macrorie 1977), this function of writing is particularly apparent. The authors, noted above, who have written about writing in relation to particular subjects (math, history, etc.), are specifically concerned with this virtue of writing, as well as with the precision of thought it tends to foster.

2. *Children can learn to read and listen beyond mere word recognition only if they regularly practice expressing their own meanings in speech and writing to themselves and others.*

Since reading and listening hold a central place in the traditional curriculum, at all levels, language-across-the-curriculum research has stressed the *reinforcing* nature of the four language modes. Martin et al. (1976) and Mary Barr et al. (1982), among others, illustrate this principle through student writing samples and by citing teachers who have improved their students' higher-level reading abilities through such methods as the reading-response journal. The scenarios to follow, such as the description of Al Lengel's "Opinion/Commentary" assignment in chapter seven, will show how children's motivation, planning, and comprehension improve when their reading becomes an occasion for expressing their opinions and for comparing their views with those of the teacher and other students. In such classrooms, reading, like the other language modes, is translated from a mere "skill"—isolated for special attention in a fragment of the school day—into a way for children to discover, and own, information on any topic. Reading also becomes a source of inspiration for the children's own writing: for example, a poem may provide a model or pattern for the children's own verse; more important, reading will provide ideas and points of view that children can argue with and embellish. The teacher can challenge the student to imagine changes in a story, or to rewrite a character because of new information added to a plot.

Perhaps the integration of the language modes most affects reading development by changing the child's view of what it means to be an author. In language-rich classrooms the children often become authors themselves, with their stories, autobiographies, essays, and reports being read to other children and published, with laminated covers perhaps, for the school library. The complex process of writing—brainstorming ideas, gathering information, testing ideas out on the page, revising, gathering more information, and so on—can give children real insight into the process followed by the authors of the books they read. When children's reading and writing, and speaking and listening, are seen as a continuum carried on between people and from person to person to person, then children can begin to identify with the writers whose works they read and can see those writers as companions. If this sounds like a grandiose way of describing the text-child relationship, that is only because for so long school communication has followed a radical model: top-down and one-way—the supposedly authoritative text (and authoritative teacher) to the supposedly ignorant child. But with the findings of the linguists and cognitive scientists concerning the essential interrelatedness of understanding and expression, clearly the conventional model is insufficient, and is being supplanted by one that recognizes and builds upon the child's knowledge. Nowhere is this new model more evident than in our view of the composing process, which we have learned to see as similar in many ways for both children and adults, neophytes and professionals. By seeing writing as an ineluctably *recursive* process (Nancy Sommers 1980), which always "turns back" on itself in messy, unpredictable ways because of the uncertain mesh between words and meanings, we have discarded the old metaphor of the gulf that lies between the genius who is "born" to write well and the child who "does it wrong" because writing is not easy for him or her. In its place we now affirm the idea of writing as craft, which can be learned by almost everyone but which never becomes easy or automatic for anyone, including professional authors. If children know this, and if children themselves are frequent writers, then those children come to appreciate the books they read for the skill and perseverance of the people who write them; moreover, these children do not feel cut off from the achievement of similar or greater mastery.

Linguistic and cognitive research has had as profound an effect on attitudes toward listening as it has had on attitudes toward reading. The old model of listening presents a quiet person who "pays attention," "takes it all in," and then "gives it back" when called on to recite or to write a test answer. This model conforms well to the radical authoritarian model of smart text/teacher and ignorant child. The best-known skill associated with this model of listening is that of "orderly and complete" notetaking, which means taking down as quickly as possible as many of the speaker's exact words as one can. The aim of such listening and recording is not thinking or knowing, but the ability to "give it back." Most students learn this model so well in their early education that they find it nearly impossible in their later years to *interpret*—that is, to relate what they see and hear to other parts of their experience—or to use spoken or written information in any other personally meaningful way. By trying to sever expression from the learning process (the classroom "so quiet you can hear a pin drop" is still an ideal in many places), teachers can make *knowing* impossible, according to the definition of knowledge developed by the cognitivists and linguists.

To nurture thought, and thus knowledge, speech and listening theorists have suggested key functions that oral communication should serve in school, at work, and at home (R. R. Allen and Robert Kellner 1984; Barbara Wood 1984), including the following:

1. Controlling: the effort to influence others or respond to others' attempts to control (e.g., bargaining, refusing)

2. Sharing feelings: expression of emotion or our response to feelings of others (e.g., anger, support)

3. Informing/responding (e.g., explaining, questioning)

4. Ritualizing: initiation or maintenance of social contact (e.g., greetings, small talk)

5. Imagining: creative interpretation of reality (e.g., storytelling, fantasy)

These writers have shown how the key functions of oral communication can be integrated across the curriculum, as well as made integral to other language modes. The following chapters will present numerous examples of talking and listening, between teacher and student and between and among students, that illustrate these key functions in action.

Of all the strategies by which teachers reinforce the other language modes through talk, no doubt the use of small groups, from pairs to nine- or ten-member teams, has received the most attention. One reason for this has been the proven importance of peer comment on the writing of both children and adults (e.g., Britton et al. 1975; Thom Hawkins 1976; Donald Graves 1983). Moreover, such groups have also allowed teachers to give children practice in performing all the key functions listed above. When students in the early grades work in groups, as in chapters three and four, the language interaction in the school can take advantage of, and really be an extension of, the group dynamics that the children learn at home and at play. That such peer interaction creates a natural and effective learning environment has been demonstrated by Britton (1970) and such others as Mike Torbe and Peter Medway (1981), Donald Rubin and Kenneth Kantor (1984), and Joan Isenberg and Evelyn Jacob (1985), whose analyses of conversations have shown how even very young children teach one another and inspire one another's creativity. Britton has also shown how such conversations gradually teach children how to take turns and share leadership. If such work is reinforced in the schools, with the teacher modeling, guiding, and supervising the interaction (e.g., Wood 1984), then all children, including the more reticent and the more outspoken, can profit from peer learning.

The teacher who uses talk to stimulate learning must tolerate—indeed, exploit—the tendency of conversation to grow associatively from topic to topic rather than to follow logically the subthemes of an idea. Since curricula tend to be organized in restrictive, carefully focused units, many teachers have shied away from encouraging discussion and conversation. But, say the cognitivists (e.g., Robert Ornstein 1975), by thwarting this associative flow, educators prohibit students from creating patterns of related ideas and images (Charles Suhor 1982) and thus make it difficult for children to give order and meaning to their experiences. One important role for the teacher in the language-rich classroom is to help children see how their flood of ideas does form coherent patterns. The teacher, in supervising conversation, can perform the analytic function of pointing out new ideas that the conversation has led to, and can ask salient questions that push children to consider apparent contradictions or new information. The teacher can also help children learn how to bring a conversation back from free brainstorming to focus on an original question, and thus how to use the insights the brainstorming has given them. In this way, teachers help their students achieve versatility as learners, speakers, and listeners, while keeping discussion within the context of the curricular program. Again, the following chapters show how specific teachers achieve these results.

3. *Children learn only if knowledge is defined in action as a dialogue, or conversation, between teacher and student, student and student, student and the text, and student and the world.*

This third consequence of language-and-learning theory means that knowledge must be redefined in the school. Where I concluded the last section by suggesting how teachers could strike a balance between formal program demands and their students' needs as learners and communicators, this section takes on what we mean by curriculum itself.

One reality of American education is that curriculum is constantly in flux. In such areas as science, math, and history, what we teach rides the winds of change in technology, politics, school finances, and standardized testing, to name a few major influences. As the "knowledge explosion" continues, the main direction in curriculum seems outward, with ever more added to what must be "covered." Witness the current concern of school districts to bring computers into the classroom and to train teachers, as well as students, to use them. What does not seem to change, however, is our sense of knowledge as a thing, like food, that exists inanimately outside the person and must be deliberately ingested in discrete bits. We expand the school day, or increase the number of separate periods or units, in order to cram into the curriculum every*thing* we want our children to be "exposed to." No wonder teachers feel overwhelmed; no wonder their frustration that they must continually move on to something else "just when things have really gotten going."

In this light, many might greet language across the curriculum as just more stuff to be crammed into the schedule. This is a natural reaction, given that most elementary curricula, like those at other levels, isolate the "language arts" as a period unto themselves and concoct a *separate content* (basal readers, spelling, and grammar worksheets, etc.) for them. Thus language is one of the dishes that make up the educational meal. Operating on this metaphor, language across the curriculum—in science, math, history, etc.—would be like adding an extra bit of salad to the meat, to the potatoes, and to the dessert. But if we accept the researchers' findings that language and learning *cannot* be separated, then the food metaphor no longer works. Or if it does, it's only because we have changed the relationships. Knowledge is not the food on the plate, or the plant growing in the field, or the food being transformed into blood and tissue; knowledge is the entire process of growth and digestion and further growth. The knowledgeable person does not merely accumulate words and sensations, but makes those elements into knowledge through analysis and imagination—through constant, intense, active building of what Vygotsky called the "web of meaning." Our idiom captures this definition of knowledge in the phrase "in the know." The person in the know is at home in his or her world. This person understands the roles, the relationships, the personalities of people; this person knows what to listen for and what to say, how to say it, and to whom. This person's knowledge is inseparable from doing. In fields of study, the person in the know is he or she of insight, the one able to put appearances together in imaginative patterns so that we can use them in new ways. This person applies language-and-learning theory in what we might call an active appreciation of the relativity of fact. That is, if knowledge—"fact"—cannot be separated from the language we use to express it, and if language, as shown earlier, changes its meaning from person to person, then the knowledgeable person does not swallow other people's explanations as fact, but takes on an open-minded, experimental attitude. He or she is always prepared to see new relationships, draw different conclusions. The more we use language, the more we learn that knowledge is a dynamic and ever-changing thing.

This language theory of knowledge, while it calls into question our conventional thinking about curriculum, conforms easily to dominant recent theories in the subjects we teach. The clearest example is science, which trusts experimentation—the systematic *search* for truth—more than it does assumptions or conclusions. Particularly in the last eighty years, science, led by Einstein, Bohr, and others, has brought about a change in what we can take for granted about the universe. With the fall of the Newtonian absolutes of time and space came a reevaluation of basic assumptions not only in science but in all fields, language study included. The result has been an increasingly open attitude toward truth; specifically, an increasing appreciation of how culture and personality shape our interpretations of reality. Unfortunately, since schools, in method and model, have tended to maintain the bits-and-pieces view of knowledge, they have been ill suited to adapt to these changes. However, when a language-across-the-curriculum attitude is brought to bear on the teaching of science, for example, emphasis shifts from isolated bits of trivia ("What is the boiling temperature of water?") to such basics of scientific method as precise observation and hypothesizing. When students write their descriptions of a swimming goldfish and then compare their descriptions with those of one another, they learn that others see differently from themselves and they learn to expand their notions of the seeable. When they are asked to speculate in writing or in a brainstorming session on how life in outer space might look—and why it would look that way—they learn to speculate, to hypothesize, in a scientific way.

Changes in other disciplines also call out for a learning-through-language approach. For example, it may have been possible at one time to teach a "standard" American history course on the formation of the federal government and the westward movement of European settlers, but with the recognition of the pluralism of our society and thus its many histor*ies*, children must now learn history as ways of interpreting events, not only as items on a time line. Children can write the histories of themselves, or they can build histories of their towns or neighborhoods from interviews and newspapers, and thus learn how historians work, and how elusive the past can be. They can understand how historians must select details and must use their imaginations to make sense of fragmentary memories and conflicting reports. Comparing their work with that of other students can teach them how to defend their conclusions and how to tell a story that is both interesting and true.

Perhaps no discipline so merits attention from a language-across-the-curriculum perspective as mathematics, since on the one hand the "facts" in the field seem so definite, yet on the other hand so few children do well. Math educators have long recognized that the abstractness of the rules and symbols and their seeming arbitrariness thwart the attempt of many to comprehend them, much less understand them. Consequently, recent theory, spurred in part by the computer revolution, has tried to subordinate the symbolic questions and give primacy to what the cognitivists would call the need to quantify and to find a language that can represent the process. In other words, mathematics has been moving toward a more inductive, "problem-solving" emphasis (e.g., Gyorgy Polya 1971), which presents to the student "real-life" situations that call for problems to be identified and quantitative solutions suggested. Often these situations don't present themselves in a conventionally mathematical way (e.g., "If you have ten cookies and divide them equally among five children, how many will each child receive?"). Rather, these situations appear nonquantitative in nature; for example, students may be asked to solve a crime, and will be given a list of suspects, a few characteristics of each, and a list of details from the scene of the crime. The goal of presenting such situations is to give students practice organizing and classifying information so that it yields a practical result. With the teacher's help, students learn to see that they cannot solve such problems without creating a symbolic language, or shorthand, as a way of keeping all the data in order and then manipulating these data in a convenient way. Such practice builds in the learner a math "sense," the basis for all further analytic reasoning; such practice also gives the child greater motivation to learn mathematical symbols and operations, which are needed to solve these practical puzzles.

Computerization demands this approach to mathematics. Because computers "speak" and "read" in mathematically precise ways, we can't use (i.e., program) them without being able to phrase and solve actual problems in a precise symbolic way that the computer can read.

In language terms, learning quantitative analysis and mathematical symbolism is language learning of a most creative kind. Thus, expressive writing in the spectator mode is vital here. As scientists, mathematicians keep notebooks of their brainstorming or test out their notions on the computer. Only through discovery, revision, and further discovery do math operations and computer programs, like poems or grant proposals, become straightforward and effective. Mathematics and computer science teachers apply these lessons by having their students keep journals, or "thinkbooks," in which they practice both putting mathematical language into their own words and speculating on mathematical solutions to nonmathematical (at least in appearance) problems.

Learning the Language: The Other Side of the Same Coin

To this point, I have talked about language across the curriculum as a way of understanding how learning can best and most fully occur in school. I have not talked about many of the things that teachers and parents frequently mean when they talk about language in the elementary grades: such things as spelling, vocabulary, and "correct" grammar. I do not mean to slight these aspects of language acquisition; indeed, my presentation has thus far dealt implicitly with them in that I have emphasized the need for a language-rich curriculum, one that involves children in a tremendous variety of language-using activities at all ages. The theory here is developmental. In a language-rich environment, where children read, listen, speak, and write as an essential way of learning, they will grow—sometimes gradually, sometimes amazingly quickly—into competent language users in every aspect of the endeavor. In particular regard to such elements as spelling, vocabulary, and syntax, the most important influence, besides direct use, appears to be modeling by others. By modeling I do not mean a teacher's standing before a class and asserting the value of correct spelling, etc. Similarly, I do not mean a teacher's testing students on arbitrary lists of words or assigning daily vocabulary and "grammar" exercises. These practices perhaps have a place in the language-rich environment, but not in place of other, more productive work.

Rather, the modeling I mean is characterized by enthusiasm directed toward personal, observable goals. For example, Jana Staton (1984) has reported the startling growth in standard English writing skills by Hispanic children whose teachers correspond *with* them in "dialogue journals." The key feature of these journals is that the teacher responds to the *content* of the journals—the children's feelings and beliefs—not their spelling, syntax, etc. Consciously or unconsciously, the student models his or her own writing on the teacher's, because the teacher is using the language in a way that shows sincere interest in the child. The very fact that the teacher is *writing* is significant modeling. Can we learn any art without the example of the person who teaches us? Consider music or painting, for example. This does not mean that teachers must be expert writers. It does mean, however, that children should have the opportunity to observe how the teacher goes about solving the challenges of composing. An easy way to do this is for the teacher to write along with the children as they keep their journals. Another is for the teacher to join with the class in composing, revising, and editing a common piece of writing—say a

letter inviting parents to back-to-school night, or a thank-you letter to
the staff of a museum that the class visited. From the teacher's example, children can learn that composing takes lots of thought and
lots of experimenting with combinations of words. This process can
show them that writing is not and is not supposed to be an easy or
"clean" art.

This emphasis on modeling suggests that we become better language users once we discover the rewarding things we can do with
words, and that our conscious attention to *how* we use words—our
spelling, syntax, usage, etc.—follows from the exciting discovery that
people we respect or love gain happiness in various ways from writing
and speaking. Conversely, for a teacher or parent to be too attentive to
mechanics of speech or writing *before* a child has made this discovery
is to inhibit the child's development as a language user. The experience of teachers at all levels who have their students keep journals, or
learning logs, corroborates this finding. Indeed, students tend to write
more coherent, fluent pieces as less attention is paid by the teacher to
their mechanical use of the language.

How well this idea of the development of writing and speaking
abilities complements the already described objectives of the language-
across-the-curriculum classroom! It means that teachers who make
writing and speaking a really integral part of each subject in the
curriculum can feel confident that they are helping their students
become better language users. Teachers at the secondary and university
levels have worried that in order to make their classes language rich,
they must "take over the job of the English teacher," meaning that
they, too, must adopt the stereotyped role of the writing teacher as
tireless seeker of spelling demons and dangling participles. These
teachers have assumed that without the grammarian's specialized
training and vocabulary, they do not know how to give their students
profitable comment on their written or spoken work. But the example
of Staton and others (e.g., Elaine Lees 1979) implies that the most
productive comments are those questions and clarifications we make
about the substance—the ideas—of the student's work, comments that
are precisely *within* the teacher's realm of knowledge. Math teachers
can comment on students' math journals because they know math;
the same is true of every other field. It is certainly true of the multiple-
subjects teacher in the elementary grades.

While teacher or parent comment is important in the development
of language-using ability, writing-process research suggests that most
of the practical benefit of writing and speaking accrues to the student
irrespective of reader/listener comment. In citing his own and others'
research of language learning by young children, Britton (1970) pointed

out that only a small fraction of babies' "practice" with words and utterances received parental or sibling "correction," or response of any kind. And as Vygotsky (1962) noted, this percentage of uncommented-on speech rises with the years, as we transform our language practice into "inner speech." By the time we are adults we seem to be formulating sentences in our minds incessantly and feel only the occasional need to express ourselves to others. We obviously operate on the principle that we are our own best teachers.

This is not to say that teacher or parent comment on children's writing or speaking necessarily stunts their learning to use these tools as well as possible. Certainly all children and adults (at least I've never heard a report to the contrary) feel encouraged and motivated by comments that show genuine appreciation and interest. Some of these comments don't even require words. Publicly displaying children's writing, requesting children to read their essays and stories aloud in class, and publishing children's writings in typed, covered books tangibly show the child that his or her words mean something to us; in specific regard to speech, nothing more encourages a child than our sincerely listening to him or her and engaging the child in true conversation. As chapter six on Cynthia Dietz's speech class will show, children can demonstrate dramatic improvement in *how well* they speak if given the opportunity to converse with a teacher about a subject of their own choosing.

Conversely, nothing may so inhibit young (or old) writers and talkers than our sensitivity to the flaws in their language. The person who picks apart our words in writing or conversation doesn't nurture our improvement—unless and until we've developed strong self-confidence in our powers of expression. Lacking this strength, we merely clam up in that person's presence and never show that person our writing. Yet teachers routinely, with conventional "good intentions," mark the errors in children's writing or correct their pronunciation and grammar, while ignoring what the children are saying. One of the great findings of Mina Shaughnessy's research with open admissions college students (1977) was that their mechanical proficiency could not improve until they had become *fluent* writers, their work nurtured in an atmosphere that patiently tolerated the mistakes they made, *so that* they would be encouraged to take ever-greater risks with a language they had yet to master. Marie Nelson's work with English as a Second Language students (1985) has provided further impressive support for this approach at the college level, while the work of Graves (1983) and others (e.g., Marcia Farr 1984) has provided continuing strong evidence among elementary students. Though teachers often feel pressured by PTAs and school boards to "attack" mechanical deficiencies immediately and relentlessly, results seem to be more thorough and lasting (e.g., Linda Reed 1984) if fluency is first in the teacher's priorities. Again, the language-across-the-curriculum classroom is the ideal place for this fluency to grow.

I am not thereby implying, however, that children should never be corrected for their misspellings or missing commas. Most children want to learn the correct spellings for the words they use and learn how to punctuate their sentences, and teachers should always take advantage of a child's "How do you spell this?" One popular way in which teachers exploit this curiosity in spelling is to have children keep daily dictionaries—growing word chests—of the words they learn. Children can also learn early on that "editing"—review of their writing for spelling, punctuation, and word choice—will be a regular *final* phase of some of the projects they work on. Much student writing should remain unedited—journals, logs, notes, games, impromptu exercises, etc.—while other writings can be taken through one or more revisions following comments by the teacher or by other students on their ideas and facts. The teacher will want to ready still other writings for classroom publication or for "official" presentation to parents or for mailing to other readers; the class can edit these writings for correctness. In this way, students will assimilate the steps in the writing process (see, e.g., Suhor 1984), and the editing will not short-circuit the child's fluency or desire to revise. Moreover, the child will come to see that misspellings and other imperfections are a *necessary* part of learning to use new words and learning new ways to speak our ideas and feelings, rather than something to be ashamed of or penalized for. Like any other learning, whether across the curriculum or throughout life, language learning will succeed if we always keep alive our thirst for adventure into the unknown, and if we have the help of others—our teachers—who, regardless of the mistakes we will assuredly make, will always applaud our courage.

References

Allen, R. R., and Robert W. Kellner. "Integrating the Language Arts." In *Speaking and Writing, K-12: Classroom Strategies and the New Research,* edited by Christopher J. Thaiss and Charles Suhor, 208-27. Urbana, Ill.: National Council of Teachers of English, 1984.

Barnes, Douglas, James Britton, and Harold Rosen. *Language, the Learner, and the School.* Harmondsworth, England: Penguin Books, 1969. Available in the U.S. through Boynton/Cook.

Barr, Mary, Pat D'Arcy, and Mary K. Healy, eds. *What's Going On? Language/Learning Episodes in British and American Classrooms, Grades 4-13.* Montclair, N.J.: Boynton/Cook, 1982.

Beyer, Barry. "Using Writing to Learn History." *History Teacher* 13 (2): 167–78, February 1980. EJ 218 614.

Britton, James. *Language and Learning.* Harmondsworth, England: Penguin Books, 1970. Available in the U.S. through Boynton/Cook.

———, et al. *The Development of Writing Abilities (11–18).* London: Macmillan Education, 1975. Available in the U.S. through the National Council of Teachers of English.

Bruner, Jerome. *Toward a Theory of Instruction.* Cambridge, Mass.: Harvard University Press, 1966.

Calkins, Lucy McCormick. *Lessons from a Child: On the Teaching and Learning of Writing.* Exeter, N.H.: Heinemann Educational Books, 1983.

Emig, Janet. *The Composing Processes of Twelfth Graders.* Urbana, Ill.: National Council of Teachers of English, 1971.

———. "Writing as a Mode of Learning." *College Composition and Communication* 28 (2): 122–28, May 1977. EJ 162 045.

———. "Non-Magical Thinking: Presenting Writing Developmentally in School." In *The Web of Meaning: Essays on Writing, Teaching, Learning, and Thinking* by Janet Emig, edited by Dixie Goswami and Maureen Butler. Montclair, N.J.: Boynton/Cook, 1983.

Farr, Marcia. "Writing Growth in Young Children: What We Are Learning from Research." In *Speaking and Writing, K–12: Classroom Strategies and the New Research,* edited by Christopher J. Thaiss and Charles Suhor, 126–43. Urbana, Ill.: National Council of Teachers of English, 1984.

Flower, Linda. "Writer-Based Prose: A Cognitive Basis for Problems in Writing." *College English* 41 (1): 19–37, September 1979. EJ 209 266.

Graves, Donald. *Writing: Teachers and Children at Work.* Exeter, N.H.: Heinemann Educational Books, 1983.

Hawkins, Thom. *Group Inquiry Techniques for Teaching Writing.* Urbana, Ill.: ERIC Clearinghouse on Reading and Communication Skills and the National Council of Teachers of English, 1976. ED 128 813.

Holsinger, Donald. "Writing to Learn History." In *Writing to Learn: Essays and Reflections on Writing across the Curriculum,* edited by Christopher Thaiss, 49–55. Dubuque, Iowa: Kendall-Hunt, 1983.

Irmscher, William F. "Writing as a Way of Learning and Developing." *College Composition and Communication* 30 (3): 240–44, October 1979. EJ 212 104.

Isenberg, Joan P., and Evelyn Jacob. "Playful Literacy Activities and Learning: Preliminary Observations." In *When Children Play: Proceedings of International Conference on Play and Play Environments,* edited by Joe L. Frost and Sylvia Sunderlin. Wheaton, Md.: Association for Childhood Education International, 1985.

Jaynes, Julian. *The Origin of Consciousness in the Breakdown of the Bicameral Mind.* Boston: Houghton Mifflin, 1977.

Jeffries-Thaiss, Ann, and Christopher J. Thaiss. "Learning Better, Learning More: In the Home and across the Curriculum." In *Speaking and Writing, K–12: Classroom Strategies and the New Research,* edited by Christopher J. Thaiss and Charles Suhor, 1–28. Urbana, Ill.: National Council of Teachers of English, 1984.

King, Barbara. "Using Writing in the Mathematics Class." In *Teaching Writing in All Disciplines,* edited by C. W. Griffin, 39–44. San Francisco: Jossey-Bass, 1982.

Lees, Elaine O. "Evaluating Student Writing." *College Composition and Communication* 30 (4): 370–74, December 1979. EJ 214 082.

Macrorie, Ken. *Telling Writing.* 2d ed. Rochelle Park, N.J.: Hayden, 1977. 4th ed., Boynton/Cook, 1985.

Martin, Nancy, et al. *Writing and Learning across the Curriculum, 11–16.* London: Ward Lock Educational, 1976. Available in the U.S. through Boynton/Cook.

Murray, Donald. *Write to Learn.* New York: Holt, Rinehart and Winston, 1983.

———. *A Writer Teaches Writing.* 2d ed. Boston: Houghton Mifflin, 1985.

Nelson, Marie. "Teaching Writing to ESL Students—A Process-Based Approach." In *WATESOL Working Papers,* vol. 2, edited by C. Meloni and G. Spanos. Washington, D.C.: Center for Applied Linguistics, 1985.

Ornstein, Robert E. *The Psychology of Consciousness.* Harmondsworth, England: Penguin Books, 1975. 2d ed., Harcourt Brace Jovanovich, 1977.

Paik, Minja, and Eugene Norris. "Writing to Learn in Statistics, Mathematics, and Computer Science." In *Writing to Learn: Essays and Reflections on Writing across the Curriculum,* edited by Christopher Thaiss, 107–18. Dubuque, Iowa: Kendall-Hunt, 1983.

Polya, Gyorgy. *How to Solve It: A New Aspect of Mathematical Method.* 2d ed. Princeton, N.J.: Princeton University Press, 1971.

Reed, Linda. "Assessing Children's Speaking, Listening, and Writing Skills." In *Speaking and Writing, K–12: Classroom Strategies and the New Research,* edited by Christopher J. Thaiss and Charles Suhor, 228–60. Urbana, Ill.: National Council of Teachers of English, 1984.

Rubin, Donald L., and Kenneth J. Kantor. "Talking and Writing: Building Communication Competence." In *Speaking and Writing, K–12: Classroom Strategies and the New Research,* edited by Christopher J. Thaiss and Charles Suhor, 29–73. Urbana, Ill.: National Council of Teachers of English, 1984.

Shaughnessy, Mina P. *Errors and Expectations: A Guide for the Teacher of Basic Writing.* New York: Oxford University Press, 1977.

Sommers, Nancy. "Revision Strategies of Student Writers and Experienced Adult Writers." *College Composition and Communication* 31 (4): 378–88, December 1980. EJ 240 356.

Staton, Jana. "Thinking Together: Interaction in Children's Reasoning." In *Speaking and Writing, K–12: Classroom Strategies and the New Research,* edited by Christopher J. Thaiss and Charles Suhor, 144–87. Urbana, Ill.: National Council of Teachers of English, 1984.

Suhor, Charles. "Semiotics." ERIC/RCS Digest series. Urbana, Ill.: ERIC Clearinghouse on Reading and Communication Skills, 1982.

———. "Thinking Visually about Writing: Three Models for Teaching Composition, K–12." In *Speaking and Writing, K–12: Classroom Strategies and the New Research,* edited by Christopher J. Thaiss and Charles Suhor, 74–103. Urbana, Ill.: National Council of Teachers of English, 1984.

Tchudi, Stephen, and Susan Tchudi. *Teaching Writing in the Content Areas: Elementary School.* Washington, D.C.: National Education Association, 1983. ED 232 211.

Torbe, Mike, and Peter Medway. *The Climate for Learning.* London: Ward Lock Educational, 1981. Available in the U.S. from Boynton/Cook.

Vygotsky, Lev S. *Thought and Language,* edited by Gertrude Vakar, translated by Eugenia Hanfmann. Cambridge: Massachusetts Institute of Technology, 1962.

Wood, Barbara S. "Oral Communication in the Elementary Classroom." In *Speaking and Writing, K–12: Classroom Strategies and the New Research,* edited by Christopher J. Thaiss and Charles Suhor, 104–25. Urbana, Ill.: National Council of Teachers of English, 1984.

Wotring, Anne, and Robert Tierney. *Two Studies of Writing in High School Science.* Bay Area Writing Project Classroom Research Study No. 5. Berkeley: University of California, 1981. ED 238 725.

Documents indexed in *Resources in Education (RIE)* are denoted by a six-digit ED (ERIC Document) number. The majority of ERIC documents are reproduced on microfiche and may be viewed at ERIC collections in libraries and other institutions or can be ordered from the ERIC Document Reproduction Service (EDRS) in either paper copy or microfiche. For ordering information and price schedules write or call EDRS, 3900 Wheeler Avenue, Alexandria, VA 22304 (1-800-227-3742).

Articles annotated in *Current Index to Journals in Education (CIJE)* are denoted by a six-digit EJ (ERIC Journal) number and may be obtained from a library collection, from the publisher, or from University Microfilms International, UMI Article Clearinghouse, 300 North Zeeb Road, Ann Arbor, MI 48106 (1-800-732-0616).

3 "You Ought to Get a Book and Do Some Research, Too": Learning through Language in Math and Science

> If you had a million dollars to spend, a million dollars more or less, to spend on anything you wanted to spend it on, and you decided to spend it on ten different things . . . , what ten things would you buy, could you buy, for a million dollars, no less, no more?

It is a Monday in October, and Carin Hauser poses this question to her twenty third-grade students at Louise Archer School in Vienna, Virginia. Then to each of them she hands a "check" for $1 million and says that now they belong to the Million Dollar Club. With the check comes a one-week assignment: to keep a notebook of their wishes and an accurate list of prices for those wishes—ten items, no less—plus some "proof" of the prices: newspaper clippings, manufacturers' lists, catalog entries, etc. Following the assignment comes a small barrage of questions: "Could we get more than ten things?" ("Sure, if they don't total more than a million dollars.") "Do they all have to be different?" ("At least ten of them do—so you'll have to find different prices in different places.") "Do we have to include the tax?" ("If you want to, but I won't require it.")

Then comes the most challenging part. "What," she asks the children, who are seated around their "tables" of four desks each, "are some things we could buy with our millon dollars?" "Ice cream!" says one, and they all laugh. "I'd buy a 727," says another. "Could you buy that for a million dollars?" asks Hauser. "Try to think how you could find out the price of a 727." Other suggestions come forth, revealing different abilities to estimate values: "an expensive concert," "a Cabbage Patch doll," "a trip around the world." "I'd have a party for everyone!" says another, and they all cheer. Then Hauser urges them to think about "important" things they could use the money for, and several suggestions come forth: "try to stop air and water pollution," "build a hospital," "give to charity."

Having used the discussion to touch on other values besides quantitative ones, Hauser now brings the talk back to mathematics, with her emphasis still on creative problem solving. "Now," she says, "where can we look for the prices of the things we'll buy?" There are some seconds of silence as the children ponder. Hauser waits for their responses. Finally, one child says, "You could look in the newspaper, at the ads." Another says, "And you could also look at the other ads, the classified ads." "That's right," says Hauser. "Where else?" "How about catalogs?" suggests a third child. "We sometimes use the Sears catalog." Hauser duly notes all the suggestions on the blackboard, thereby honoring the children's contributions and encouraging the children to use the suggestions as guides for their search.

When they seem to have run out of ideas, Hauser produces one of her own. Holding up an issue of the *Washington Post,* she turns to the business section and within that to the listings for the New York Stock Exchange. "I was thinking," she says, "that one thing you might want to buy would be stock in a corporation, and this is the part of the newspaper where the latest prices of stocks are listed every day." From here, she explains a bit about prices per share, enough to show the children how they could begin to understand the listings.

In the last phase of the teacher-led dialogue, Hauser asks the students to suggest the math skills that they would need to do the ten-item, million-dollar assignment. "Addition," "subtraction," "multiplication," "division" come in rapid succession. To these Hauser adds, "How about estimating?" in reference to exercises the class has been doing recently. "Oh yeah!" says one child, and several others nod vigorously, as they begin to see how they might apply their study.

In Carin Hauser's class, both math and science are learned in this highly interactive, language-rich fashion. As this lesson illustrates, the conventional mathematics of individual computation will eventually arise out of this assignment, but in a more realistic, *inductive* way than that provided by the usual assignment in the math workbook. What might in most classrooms be an abstract exercise becomes in this situation a tantalizing class project, with each child anticipating his or her own discoveries, as well as those of the others. Indeed, what makes this project particularly exciting is that it does not seem like a "math problem" at all, but an opportunity to solve a puzzle of one's own devising. The mathematics arises inductively out of the child's incentive to make the prices match the magical figure of one million. For the children who are already able to manipulate such operations as multiplication and division, the assignment would still offer a challenge. For those who are just learning their multiplication tables, the million-dollar problem would let them apply what they know and give them incentive to learn more. For all the children, this problem provides an effective way of teaching them *how big* such numbers as 1,000,000 really are—an awareness all of us could use as we try to understand such concepts as budgets and populations.

By creating a realistic problem of this sort, Hauser is actually teaching an interdisciplinary lesson in reading (e.g., the different sections of the newspaper) and social studies (e.g., the consideration of social projects on which to spend the money). When mathematics, like other subject matters, moves away from prepackaged drills and toward solving realistic or imaginative problems, it inevitably becomes multidisciplinary, since every real issue cuts across all disciplines. One attendant virtue of this is that it enables teachers to meet curricular objectives in several areas through single projects.

In such an environment, mathematics becomes intimately involved with language. Hauser's using the students as her principal resource for ideas and examples necessitates her giving the students frequent practice in questioning, interpreting questions, and speaking within a large group on a problem-solving task. Solving the various parts of the problem will also require their reading and interpreting some unfamiliar, "adult" texts, including newspapers, magazines, and catalogs. This particular problem will not require much writing by the students, though they will no doubt be writing and revising lists of possible items, plus organizing all their data—items, prices, "proofs"— in an understandable format.

On the same morning that she presents the Million Dollar Club, Hauser also engages the students, divided into two groups of somewhat differing preparation, in other math activities that require group interaction and a more substantial amount of composing. She leads one group of fifteen, the "blue liners," in a conceptual exercise on multiplication. Standing before the students, who are gathered on the carpet in one corner of the room, she drops a handful of blocks into a metal can. She asks the children to listen and to venture guesses at the number of blocks she is dropping. The children raise their hands to guess. She repeats the action several times, each time using the same number of blocks. Then she asks the multiplication question: how many sounds have they heard altogether?

Again, her method is inductive, challenging the students to think from the particular instance to the abstract idea. These children are just beginning to learn multiplication tables, and this lesson is meant to show them the vital connection between the real problem and the mathematical symbolic operations we can use to solve it. By using the entire group to solve the demonstrated problem, she is also giving the children a social incentive to solve it; the game gives them the incentive to learn the arithmetic tools.

The next step in the lesson logically follows. Hauser asks the children to suggest problems of their own—situations that can be resolved through the same tools. The children think for a few moments; then several raise their hands. As a child states a problem, everyone in the group tries to solve it. When someone arrives at the correct answer, Hauser proceeds to the next analytical step: she asks the child how he or she arrived at the answer. Again, the children become more aware of the mental process of translating actual situations into problems that mathematics can solve. By making it necessary that the children listen to understand the problem and then express their processes in words for each other, she makes the learning process conscious. This method also makes it possible for her to learn immediately how a child may be having difficulty with a concept. (A variation on this model is to have the children keep logs of how they solve problems or understand scientific formulas. This technique allows the child and the teacher to see where the child is having a tough time understanding.)

The lesson with the blue liners ends with Hauser's assignment that each child compose ten multiplication problems of his or her own, including "three good word problems that require multiplication." Later, I ask three of the children if they like to write their own problems. They concur, adding that they like their own problems better than those from a book "because when you write your own problems, you learn how to write them and you learn why things go where they do."

As the blue liners work on their assignments, the other five children, the orange liners, work both independently and in pairs on a different task. This is a more advanced group, with the children able to do simple multiplication and division with some ease. By keeping the tasks of the two groups different and by not being bound to a sequence of assignments in a workbook, Hauser has minimized the children's feeling that one group is "behind" the other. There is no evidence of the common distinction between the advanced learner, who is given more creative work, and the "slower" learner, who does programmed drills (or vice versa). While the fifteen create their word problems for each other, the five first solve a multistep problem that requires adding, subtracting, multiplying, and dividing; then each child creates his or her own problem on the same model.

The final step for this group is to exchange and solve one another's problems. As with the blue liners' work, the value of this problem-creating assignment is as much communicative and social as it is mathematical. As every teacher knows, creating problems for others to solve makes one sensitive to the perceptions and abilities of others, just as it forces one to think more strenuously about the concepts one is trying to teach. For both groups, the creative composing task will push the children to imagine problems that they *cannot* yet solve, as well as those they can. For example, in creating their own multi-operational problems, the advanced group comes up with numbers that will not divide evenly and with negative answers that will then need to be multiplied. These results challenge the students to go beyond their current knowledge.

The last part of the morning in Carin Hauser's class is spent on science; specifically, on the students' developing research projects on dinosaurs. The class has been working about a week on the assignment, which will result in every child's preparing an illustrated booklet. Each child has chosen his or her "own" dinosaur (almost all the choices are different) and has been taking notes from the many books in the "dinosaur library," most of which have been loaned to the class by the children themselves.

This research period begins, as have others, with the whole class discussing "research questions" posed by its members. One questioner is David, who's having difficulty finding information on his choice, the Trachydon. Immediately, two others tell David of books where, in the search for their own dinosaurs, they've found the Trachydon. Other questions are similar and lead to similar kinds of help. Hauser then asks the children if they have been using the indexes and the tables of contents. Most nod their heads or murmur affirmatively. She tells them the researcher's trick of "reading around" in books, as well as reading the pages referred to by the index or contents pages. She tells them that frequently they'll find good information where they don't expect to. Two of the children relate instances when that occurred for them.

Before dismissing the group to continue on their individual searches, Hauser asks them to suggest why the group discussions of research are useful. Quickly, three ideas come forth: (1) the group gives help when "you ask for it," (2) "you might someday have a problem that someone else has today," and (3) "you might hear someone say something that will help you now." These responses are gratifying to Hauser because, as she tells me later, one of her hardest tasks with these third graders is to help them learn to listen. "It's a real sign of progress," she says, "when they want to add to, embellish, what someone else has said, or to answer thoughtfully another child's question." Consequently, she places great emphasis on working in groups, large and small, in her class.

Though the products of the dinosaur research will be unique to each child, the spirit of mutual help pervades every aspect of the project. During the half hour following the research discussion, each child follows a different pattern of movement: from the bookshelves to his or her desk—where the child seeks information from the chosen book and jots down data—then to the "library" again or to another child's desk—where one child asks the other if he or she has found the answer to a specific question. The curious kibbitz, wondering what startling facts others have come across today, while Hauser answers individuals' questions or asks a child how he or she is progressing.

The children do not conduct their study haphazardly, going from book to book and taking down information at random. Rather, they work from lists of questions that they have generated: "How tall was the Tyrannosaurus Rex? How many teeth did it have? Where on earth did it live?" For every question a child answers (all data are kept in a notebook), another, it seems, is added, usually to accommodate new data *already* discovered, or because another child, out of curiosity, asks it of the researcher. One of the many ways in which the children work together on the project is by reading their questions and answers to each other. In this way, children add to their lists the good questions that their friends have asked; meanwhile, they continually build one another's self-esteem, as each child becomes the "expert" on his or her part of the entire dinosaur project.

Each morning's research ends with the systematic sharing of facts by the four to five children at each grouping of desks. Hauser designates the first person to share; then each child takes a brief turn describing his or her discoveries for the day. She instructs the children to evaluate themselves on their hour's work, scoring their notebooks from 1 to 5, with 5 meaning "I learned something new and I did lots of looking." Each self-score is to be followed by the child's statement of why he or she deserved that score. Hauser wants the children once again to become conscious of their learning; moreover, the assessment provides the children with a day-by-day record of their progress. Most of the children give themselves 5s, and for most this is an accurate assessment. If nothing more, the score reflects their excitement and their sense of accomplishment. As David said to me earlier, as he carried a book from the library to his desk, "This is a great book on the Trachydon. You ought to get a book and do some research, too."

The dinosaur project demonstrates that under the heading of science, much learning goes on in Carin Hauser's class that could also and equally well be called history, communication, writing, and reading. As with the mathematics learning in this class, the inductive way of teaching, by which the children gain knowledge on their own incentive and with one another's aid, is always language rich and is therefore always interdisciplinary. Note also that the science learning consists not only of biological/archeological "facts," even though the children do find a remarkable amount of such data. The most important scientific principles that this research method teaches are principles of investigation: the children learn how to look and how to listen; they learn how to cooperate with other learners; and they learn that the patient, careful search for knowledge is almost always rewarded with discovery. These children may not yet be in the traditional science laboratory, but they are growing adept at the basic skills they will need there.

Carin Hauser Comments on Her Teaching: Hatching Experts

Jan wanted to find out about the duckbilled dinosaur. She started her research by listing these questions in her notebook:

1. How do scientists know duckbill has the bill?
2. How did duckbill get away from danger in the water?
3. What was the closest relative of the duckbill?
4. How many bones of duckbill have been found?
5. What is the duckbill's main diet?
6. Why does duckbill have two names?
7. Why does duckbill need a duck bill?
8. How big are duckbill's footprints?
9. Where are duckbill's fossils found?
10. How long are duckbill's teeth?

These questions directed Jan's research. Along with her third-grade classmates, who were investigating other dinosaurs, she read many books and magazines in order to resolve the questions that puzzled and intrigued her. She also added more questions to her list, questions that showed her growing expertise.

Through reading, writing, and sharing with each other, my students become true experts on their topics. They have no difficulty creating the main vehicle through which they share their knowledge with others, their published books. Through the research process, they become experts; thus, they can write with a great depth of information. Before Jan started her first draft of her dinosaur book, she wrote in her journal:

> I feel I know enough about duckbill to write two different reports. Doing research was long and tiring. Duckbill is very interesting. I learned a lot. If someone said, "Duckbill had only 25 teeth!" I would know that person didn't study duckbill, because he had 2,000 teeth!

Jan wrote her book about duckbill with imagination, humor, and the voice of an expert. She was able to do so because she immersed herself in her topic through her reading and talking with her fellow researchers. This is the beginning of Jan's book:

> If you went back into time onto a marshy shore in North America and you saw something like a duck swimming towards you, but when it stood up, thirty feet long, 16 feet high, it did not look like a duck except the bill, you actually would have seen duckbill, the duck billed dinosaur.

During the course of our dinosaur study, twenty other children, like Jan, became paleontological experts. Can the Smithsonian boast that many paleontologists who daily encourage and motivate each other in their research?

Our dinosaur studies took place in the fall. In January, we started a social studies unit on Native Americans. As a group, we read and talked about the history of the Native Americans in our country. From a broad base of common knowledge, the children set out to investigate research topics of their own, reading, viewing appropriate filmstrips, and visiting local museums in order to find out as much as possible about their Indian topics. They also used each other as resources. I am always tickled to see students list each other as "sources" in their research notes.

I found that my students' research skills became more and more sophisticated as the year progressed. Yes, they were using the card catalog, cross-references in indexes and encyclopedias, and the periodical guides, all skills that we traditionally teach through basal reading programs or library studies. But these third graders went far beyond the limited scope of such skills into the real "stuff" of research. They read and listened and wrote and talked in order to answer their own questions, not somebody else's, to find information, and to understand their topics. Their research was a form of problem solving, and like problems and puzzles, the research was not without its difficult points. For instance, a third grader often would ask, "How much of this big book should I read to find out about the Hopi Indians?" Too often, young children are intimidated by the bigger texts that might hold valuable information for them. I tried to help the children figure out which parts of the text they needed to read, and I also helped them make sense of complex information. Sometimes I even read parts of a text aloud to a small group or to an individual, and we discussed the information to make sense of it. The children made their own notes in their research notebooks; these notes reflected facts and data and, more important, the information they chose as significant to their search.

As the children grew more adept as researchers, they also became more decisive about choosing the form for sharing their information. With the end of the school year approaching, I still have a few students who write reports that are no more than an accumulation of facts, but this kind of writing is in the minority. Most of the children choose a form through which they can boast a real expertise on their topics.

The following excerpt is from the beginning of "Seven Sleeps with Running Elk," David's story about a Sioux boy. He had a particular interest in that tribe because his mother had grown up in Sioux City.

First Sleep (Mon.)

I rise with the sun. (That is a Sioux rule—to wake with the sun in the morning and go to bed with it at night.)

I, Running Elk, am 8 winters and 7 moons old. Once again I have spent the night in dreams of the buffalo hunt. Will I never be 10 winters old?

Like all Sioux boys, I have slept in a loose buckskin shirt that hangs below my knees. I wear this shirt day and night. I wear no underclothing.

I also wear a small beaded pouch in the shape of a decorated snake. This pouch holds a piece of my umbilical cord from the time of my birth. It is strong magic to protect me and I will wear it all my life.

I slip on my moccasins and go straight to my breakfast place in the tepee.

Mother has prepared a bowl of soup and boiled buffalo. Other things I like are: wild rice, beans, turnips, cactus buttons, choke-cherries, gooseberries, squaw corn, birds and your favorite and mine—buffalo meat! Sometimes, I have fish which I catch with a hook made from a mouse's ribs. And, if I do all my chores, I get a special treat called "Wasna." This is a cake of ground buffalo and wild berries.

I think I hear Grandfather calling me to gather wood for the fire. It will be a long day, as Sioux children have many responsibilities. I also have to invite neighbors to the lodge, drive the horses to water, and spend extra time training my pony for that moment of truth—the buffalo hunt!

David's story reflected not only his expertise (he was very comfortable with his new knowledge), but also his excitement and pride in the whole process of his research. His book was full of treasures: real information, voice, honesty, and humor.

The children's research efforts took time. We spent about six weeks on the research and writing part of our Indian unit. As they read and talked about their topics, the children started to explore different ideas for sharing their knowledge. Class discussions on form allowed the students to see that they had choices, and their choices eventually evolved quite naturally.

In the Indian and dinosaur studies, the children had access to a variety of resources for their studies. In May, my class and I embarked on a different kind of project: we tried hatching chickens. I learned about chicken embryology alongside the students—I had vague recollections of a similar project during high school, but the details had long since escaped me. We had only a few books from the public library and my 4-H Leader's Guide for our book resources. Inside the incubator were our fourteen objects of study; we could weigh them and candle them (hold them up to light to see the shadow of the developing organs and blood vessels), but the children really couldn't "see" what was happening inside the eggs. My objective for the unit was for the children to learn about the development of the embryo, and I knew this would involve some unusual vocabulary for them. Because of our limited resources, I was curious to see how much depth there would be to the children's learning.

The children kept journals in which they recorded what we talked about each day as well as the observable development of the embryos. Most of the children's journals became a record not only of their study of the embryology of chickens, but also of their growth as active participants in class discussions. This was not a "hands-on" unit like our science units; what the children learned was mostly from class discussions. When questions were asked that no one could answer, we checked our books. At times, we could only speculate on the answers, using information we knew to be true in order to guess.

Here are some entries from Erin's journal:

> April 26 Are they gooey, squishy, and soft inside? Has the heart started to form yet? How come they're all dirty? Is the moisture inside? Do they have feelings yet? NO
>
> April 27 No. 8 egg—2 oz. No. 1 egg—1 7/8 oz. How come it weights less 3 days after?
>   amniotic sac
>   white—albumen
>   little bubble—blastodisc
> When does the heart start to develop? 12 days? NO.
>
> May 1 Talked about journals. Ha-ha! We found out what the eggs weighed. We talked about journals. Still, how come egg No. 8 never changed its weight? Is the shell going to turn brown?
>   We looked inside the egg. It looked like one of them had a heart. One of them was moving. One looked like it had an eye. How come Ms. Hauser cracked open an unfertilized egg? How did she know it was not fertilized?

May 3 Today nothing really happens except got a little bigger. (Sorry I didn't have a lot to write about.) Today beak opens and closes. Goosebumps.

May 15 Today me and Sandra found one egg cracked. You could see its beak and feathers. It was chirping. Some of the eggs rolled around. Someone told me that is a sign of life. I mean life outside of the shell. The feathers aren't downy yet. They—the feathers look dry and gooshy.
PLEASE MAKE THE EGGS HATCH
Later: When we came in from recess—the hole on No. 2 got as big as a walnut and 1/2. Before lunch it was about as big as a jelly bean.
After: I saw the wing moving and its beak. Names for Egg No. 2: Early Bird, Willy, Miss H. No. 2
"Egg 2 has hatched."

I was surprised to note that Erin tried to keep track of new, specialized vocabulary. This was vocabulary that we used during our discussions of the changes taking place inside the eggs, vocabulary that was unfamiliar to the children. Erin's journal became a place where she recorded much more than new words, though; she recorded answers to her own questions, as well as her feelings and reactions.

The children chose a variety of forms for sharing what they knew about embryology: illustrated books, articles for *Ranger Rick,* letters to uncles, question-and-answer brochures. One child wrote "The Journal of a Farm Girl." Erin chose to write from the viewpoint of a reporter, narrating the events of hatching day.

EXTRA . . . EXTRA . . . 111's LATEST NEWS
It all started when . . .
"Erin, could you please move the chicken box off the back table?" said Miss H.
I moved the box on a chair. When I put the box down I heard loud chirping coming from the incubator.
"Miss Hauser," I cried, "I heard some chirping!"
"Check again," said Miss H.
Sandy walked to the table and peered through the incubator.
"Erin," she whispered, "there's a hole in one of the eggs!"
"Sandy, stop the kidding," I whispered.
"Look for yourself," she said. I looked in. I saw a hole about as big as a jellybean. "Miss Hauser," Sandy and I called, "there's a hole in one of the eggs."
Soon 25 people rushed toward us forming into a line. Miss H. peered in and said in a cheerful voice, "Erin and Sandy are right."

With these projects, as with the dinosaur and Indian units, the children not only expressed their expertise on the topics they studied, but they wrote with a voice that touches, and sometimes surprises, the reader. The voice—indeed, the entire writing—evolved naturally out of intense study done from a third grader's perspective, at a third grader's pace. All of the writing is memorable.

During the school year, we hatched more than chickens in Room 111. I witnessed the growth of experts. These experts learned to be aggressive questioners and researchers. They also learned to help each other in the process, from helping another student find a book to responding to a first draft. And so Room 111 hatched an entire cadre of embryologists, paleontologists, and anthropologists.

4 Tales from the Author's Office: Language and Learning in First Grade

Clifton School stands atop a green hill that overlooks the tiny nineteenth-century town of Clifton, in western Fairfax County, some thirty miles southwest of Washington, D.C. To reach Mary Browning Schulman's first-grade classroom, I pass through the original half of the school, built early this century, and into the modern wing, built in the last decade. Like the town, whose oldest buildings preserve the rural past but whose residents, in increasing proportion, consist of Washington commuters who inhabit the new developments that ring the town, the school clings to its roots even as it responds to present ideas and their technological symbols. In the common workspace surrounded by the classrooms of the new wing, a computer hugs one wall, while cabinets of crayons, paste, and tempera guard another. Children's paintings cover the other walls: some are of flowers and animals, some of robots and extraterrestrials.

Having arrived early, accompanied by my five-year-old son, Christopher, I admire the art while waiting for Schulman to conclude her conference with a parent. The children have not yet arrived; the school is quiet, ready. Even in this recent addition, I feel caught up in a comfortable tradition, as the old school in the old town begins the new day.

There is nothing quintessentially old, or new, about Mary Schulman's teaching. This is first grade, so the children are young, but they are not "new" to school—most of them have been in a school environment two years or more. In basic terms, *what* Schulman teaches is not new either; the children read, they write, they add and subtract, and they learn (one trusts) to be good citizens of the school while at the same time developing their uniqueness.

What may be new, or at least different from the stereotype of the first-grade class, is *how* these goals are met. And how these goals are met depends, at least in part, on relatively new assumptions that teachers such as Schulman bring to their work each day. Having studied researchers from Britton to Graves, Schulman assumes, for example, that her students bring with them to first grade years of practical experience with language, hence much practical expertise in English grammar, plus some knowledge of spelling. More important, she makes the basic assumption that children bring with them a great fascination with words, a yearning to communicate, and a yearning to understand. She knows that with opportunity and encouragement, children not only can read and write, talk and listen, but they can grow to perceive themselves as "readers," "writers," "speakers," and "listeners." The distinction between ability and self-awareness of those abilities is crucial for the child's sense of self, and in classrooms like Schulman's the distinction is made deliberately, carefully, and emphatically.

In Schulman's class, everyone is an author, and it is authorship, with its connotations of *authority* and *authenticity,* that distinguishes the language work in this environment from the more passive, fragmented "reading," "writing," etc., that occurs in the conventional first grade. In Schulman's class, reading, writing, speaking, and listening all contribute to authorship. In this environment, people read to comprehend more than just combinations of letters and words, as they do in many first grades. Here the goals are more ambitious. The children read as authors do: to learn new things, to learn what other people think about things, and to learn how people say things. On any given morning, as on this November morning when Christopher and I visit, Schulman's students will read (or listen to) three basic types of texts: the "books" and journal entries written by their classmates, published books for children written by adults, and basal texts that the children read and analyze in small-group workshops. Each type of reading contributes to the idea that "everyone is an author." The children read one another's original drafts because of the mutual reward received by being and having a good audience. They do this because they have already learned that authors help one another in this way. As soon as a child finishes reading his or her story to another student or to a group, the author tells what he or she likes best about the manuscript and then asks for questions and comments, as these are the two response methods by which writers learn about their work. In addition to each other's writings, the children read published books because they want to learn new things, new ways of imagining, and new ways of writing. Though the children may not yet conceptualize these reasons, they act on them by adapting to their own work the styles or techniques of the professional writers they encounter. For example, Kimberly tells the class that the "zigzag" printing style in her own book on autumn was something she saw and liked in a book about Halloween. The children are also attracted to the small library of published books in the classroom because of the veneration in which the authors are held. Every Monday sees a new "Author of the Week"—this week Stan and Jan Berenstain are featured—and the children bring in books by these authors to display and share during the week.

The way in which groups of students in reading workshops read and talk about basal stories mirrors to a great extent the way Schulman wants the children to pay attention to their own and each other's writing. Schulman will project, or display on newsprint, an extended passage from a story, and the group will begin the workshop by reading the passage aloud in unison. Then each child in turn will read a section of the passage and identify particular words to which Schulman points. Schulman will then consider the text in various ways. She'll point out new or difficult words and ask the children for other words they'd like repeated or defined. She'll ask them for questions about the plot or about relationships of characters—anything they are puzzled about or would like to comment on. She'll also point out grammatical features that the students might adapt to their own stories: using quotation marks to show dialogue, for example. Finally, she'll ask them, as she does when they listen to one another's writings, to suggest a clearer or "better" way of saying something:

> *Schulman:* How would you change the text?
> *Gavin:* I think it should say "said the duck," not "he said," because it's easier to understand.

By treating the published text in this way, she reinforces for the children the idea that all texts, even printed ones, are revisable. The workshop also allows the children to practice the kinds of analysis and response that are appropriate when considering each other's work. Another function of the group is that it allows the airing of different opinions:

> *Mark:* I think you could say "he said" because it says "the duck" in the line before.

Better than any lecture by the teacher, this reiterated experience teaches these six-year-old authors about the variety of audiences and about alternative ways of viewing.

When "everyone is an author," the milieu of authorship, even in first grade, can be so invigorating, so inherently exciting, that the members of the community seek every opportunity to engage in its routines. During the ample amount of unstructured time in which the children can work on their writings-in-progress, students continually seek out one another as listeners to their drafts, or ask for comments on the pictures to accompany the stories, or invite other children to join them in reading books from the Author of the Week display. Christopher, a year younger than the regular class members, is quickly made a part of the community through invitations to listen to, look at, and talk about the prized prose of different individuals. Every child in the class seems proud of his or her work and eager to share it.

The prestige of authorship in Mary Schulman's room is tangibly symbolized. As in Carin Hauser's class, Schulman has arranged the desks in "tables" of five or six to make small-group workshops easier. In addition, an assortment of chairs of different sizes and designs forms a kind of reading room beside the Author of the Week display, and these are available for impromptu pairs or threes that want a bit of privacy for their literary conversations.

One special symbol of authorial prestige is the "Author's Office"—a brown cardboard playhouse with a door and a window. Within it are a chair, a desk, and a lamp. The "office" dominates the back wall of the room. Every day a different child is "in residence" there, for as much privacy as he or she wishes. Of course, since the children much prefer one another's company—and attentiveness—the "author" spends little time there. Still, holding the office is a real source of pride. The boy who holds the honor on the day we visited invites both Christopher and me into "his" office to try out "his" chair and desk.

Perhaps the central routine of the morning is Sharing Time. About ten o'clock, the entire class gathers on the carpet near the Author's Office, and one child sits in a small rocker and reads aloud from his or her writing. As they listen, the children munch on midmorning snacks—the granola bars, pretzels, or cheese cubes they've brought from home just for Sharing Time.

On this morning, Stephanie reads her current work, a Christmas morning story that she has written and illustrated on both sides of an 11″ x 16″ poster. As she reads, she holds up the poster so all can see her drawings. When her reading is concluded, she, according to practice, asks for comments and questions:

> *Kevin:* How did you get the idea to write about Christmas?
> *Stephanie:* It's coming soon. I knew that Santa would be here with lots of toys.
> *Mary:* I like the way you did the sequins on the tree.
> *Kimberly:* So do I. I like the story, too.
> *Mary:* Is that you in the picture?
> *Stephanie:* No. Santa. We aren't there, because we went out to eat. I didn't say it was Santa because I didn't have time.
> *Mary:* What would you add if you could?
> *Stephanie:* I'd add a note that says, "Dear Santa—We're not here."

When the questions and comments conclude, all the children applaud the author. Sharing Time continues with two or three other children reading their writings aloud. About once a week each child has a turn.

The questions and comments take similar form from author to author. In every session, some praise is given, either specific—"I like the way you did the sequins on the tree"—or general—"I like the author and the story." In addition, questions of clarification are asked—"What is that a picture of in the corner?" Other children generally ask the author questions about the source—"Where did you get your idea?"—and questions about further details—"What do you still want to add?" If the children don't ask one of these questions (rarely the case), Schulman poses these questions, since an important element of her teaching of the writing process is that the children keep in mind both the sources and the potential of their writing.

The question categories of Sharing Time provide an effective model for the children's thoughts about their own evolving stories as well as for the frequent sharing of drafts in impromptu pairs and threes. This model also reflects the analytic reading the children do in their workshops. Moreover, as the communal centerpiece of the morning, Sharing Time emphasizes the purposeful conviviality that is an essential element of Schulman's definition of authorship.

Clearly, in this classroom language is an instrument of joy, a brilliant gift to be continually given from one child to another. Moreover, the gift is given beyond the classroom as well. The projects on which the children work this morning will become in the next days small books with tempera-painted covers that are laminated with clear adhesive, while the texts themselves will be typed by parent aides on fresh paper, on which the children will copy their illustrations. These books will then become part of the school library, and the children will become potential Authors of the Week in some future first-grade class.

In this chapter I've chosen to emphasize how language activities cohere under a single concept—authorship—that builds both community and personality within the primary classroom. I have not focused here on that function of language stressed elsewhere in the book; namely, its essentiality in learning subject matters across the curriculum. That such learning is going on in projects such as I've described here should be clear, though the morning's curriculum is not divided into familiar subject units. For the book publication enterprise, each child works on a subject of his or her choosing. These subjects span a whole curriculum of subject areas for these children: friends, pets, important days, hobbies, machines. Through their sharing with one another, the children will learn about a multitude of things. A case in point: Kevin, one of the few students in this once-rural school who still lives on a farm, loves farm equipment and other machines. His book contains pictures of some of these machines and sentences about them. He shows Christopher and me his book, and we, as part of the group, ask him the appropriate questions. Hence, we see and learn about tractors, tractor trailers, bulldozers, forklifts, and seeders. Kevin is the classroom expert on this area of the curriculum. As he reads his work, he teaches others. As others question him, they push him to extend the frontiers of his knowledge.

Mary Browning Schulman Comments on Her Teaching: "It's Probably More Than a Young Girl Should Know"

Kirstin sits cross-legged in the child-size director's chair and responds, "Well . . . I've been a writer for a long time. I like writing poems. They're easy for me." Kirstin, a six-year-old first grader, responds confidently to another child's question after reading her latest poem, "It's Spring," during Sharing Time.

Kirstin has been a writer since the first day of kindergarten. On that warm August day, Kirstin sat down at the round writing table, when her teacher invited a few children to write whatever they knew how to write, and filled the page with these words:

STOP KIRSTIN DOGS
IN TOO ME UP NO TODDY
PAT CAT BALL
DOG YOU RAT TODD MAN

Her teacher, on returning to the writing table, must have appeared somewhat astonished by the writing. Kirstin patted her arm and quickly responded, "That's okay, Teacher . . . it's probably more than a young girl should know!" It was more than the teacher expected any young child to be able to write upon entering the world of elementary school. I know because I was Kirstin's kindergarten teacher, and I am now her first-grade teacher.

Kirstin is like many children who enter school believing that they can write. They are able to hold a crayon or pencil, draw pictures, and possibly produce some form of written expression.

During Kirstin's kindergarten school year, I encouraged her and her classmates' attempts to experiment with writing. I responded to their writing and often questioned them about things I wanted to know more about or that I didn't understand. Modeling questions and responses—such as "Read what you wrote," "Tell me more about . . . ," "This isn't clear to me. Explain what you mean," "Does that make sense?"—helped the children think about clarifying, adding to, and evaluating what they wrote. Gradually many of the same questions and responses were adopted by the children as they listened to each other's writings during Sharing Time. As they wrote and as they talked about their writings, they began to think about others' viewpoints. A sense of audience began to develop as they listened to each other's writings. One day when Jennifer read her story to the class during Sharing Time, someone asked her the name of her cat. She responded, "I should tell my cat's name 'cause some people might not know."

Providing these kindergarten children with the opportunity to generate writing and to talk about their writing in a short conference was but one way to help them explore writing. Listening to books written by professional authors provided another occasion for the children to respond to and question written language. In addition, it also exposed them to a rich variety of language models. In what I refer to as a "literature conference," questioning went beyond who was in the story and what happened when. When I first began reading aloud to the children, I modeled my thinking process as a reader interacting with the story or text. Soon we began to work through it as a group. The children began summarizing what the story text was about as I read, discussing things that were not clear to them (i.e., monitoring to make sense), predicting what might come next, and using background knowledge and new information to form their own opinions and ideas.

When I followed the children from kindergarten to first grade, I decided to design my reading program to meet, support, and extend the development of the children's writing abilities. I was aware of the pressures of administrators, colleagues, and parents to teach reading through the basal text program, and like many teachers, I was cognizant of the shortcomings of the basal texts. Since these children, as kindergarteners, were capable of writing more meaningful text and using more complex sentence patterns than the basal text, my asking them to read the same word repeatedly seemed an insult to their intelligence. When the children began to read the basal text, I did not want them to assume that any failure on their part to understand or make sense of the text meant there was some deficit in their understanding; I wanted them to be aware of the shortcomings that resided in the reading matter. When children are made to read such conversations as "Good morning, Buffy. Good morning, Mack. Good morning, Buffy. Good morning, Mack. Good morning, Buffy and Mack," they might have little incentive to read books on their own if they think that such reading is all that school has to offer.

Early in September, I began using a reading conference quite similar to the writing conference and the literature conference. I had the children read from the basal text independently, and our conference did not include using the questions in the teacher's manual. Prior to the actual reading conference, I met with the group to introduce new vocabulary from the basal text and to set the purpose for reading. The children read the text on their own and returned later in the morning or the next day to discuss the text. The reading conference often began with the children telling what they liked about the basal story (what had happened). Next, they asked questions about what they were still curious to know or what they didn't understand. Finally, they asked questions of the basal text author(s) and made suggestions.

The reading conference provided an opportunity for children to apply some of the same evaluative standards to the basal texts that they applied to their own writings and the writings of professional authors, as demonstrated in this discussion.

> *Teacher:* What did you like in this story?
> *Child 1:* I like how he makes Mack carry the sign and balloons . . . and how he made Mack write on the balloons.
> *Child 2:* I liked how the author used an exclamation point after "Lost" and "Buffy" on the balloon. You know he means lost and wants Buffy.
> *Child 3:* I like how he asked a question and then answered it [referring to the text: "Was Mack lost? Mack was lost!"].
> *Teacher:* What is it that you're still curious about knowing?
> *Child 4:* Back here I'd ask why all the balloons are the same [referring to height in the air]. He [Mack] let go at different times, so some should be higher, not the same like here.
> *Child 5:* I'd ask where they go. I know it says they went up to the hill, but I want to know after that.
> *Teacher:* [Turning back to first page in story] I want to know why Mack walked into the high grass in the first place to put the sign up. It doesn't seem like the best place for it.
> *Child 5:* Maybe he didn't realize he'd get lost.

The reading conference helped the children begin to predict and reflect on the story's content, to search for clarifications and elaborations, and to accept the responsibility for interpreting and constructing their own meaning. As makers of language, they were not intimidated by written language—not even when that written language was part of a published basal text. They had become active writers and readers intent on creating meaning. They had become aware of the choices facing them and the strategies they could use to get their meanings across, and like Kirstin, many of these first graders had come to regard themselves as veteran writers.

Reference

Early, Margaret, Elizabeth K. Cooper, and Nancy Santeusanio. *Sun Up*. New York: Harcourt Brace Jovanovich, 1983.

5 Being Normal, Being Labeled: Language and the Learning-Disabled Student

It is October, and the classroom is bright and beautiful. The early autumn sun glints off the still-green leaves of the maple just outside, turning the window into an impressionist pattern of gold and chartreuse. Along the windows, on a slate ledge, grow philodendrons and a collection of sugar crystals, each sample marked with a child's name. Creatures of another sort stand beside them: strange clay figurines, each distinct, each again labeled by the children. These make up a fantastic menagerie inspired by Dr. Seuss's *If I Ran the Zoo,* as announced by the colorful poster behind the figurines.

Also by the window, Alice Howe, teacher's aide, carefully stirs a hot saucepan of sugar syrup, makings for more crystals, while seven children peer at the notebooks on their desks, their pencils moving in hushed counterpoint to Howe's stirring of the sugar. The children's teacher, Elly Uehling, is also writing, her gaze intent on the page.

Every morning begins with the journals. In this, the beginning of the second month of school, these nine and ten year olds have already become independent journal keepers, no longer needing their teacher's prompts of "things to write about." At first, she had given them suggestions: something special that happened to you, something that made you afraid, families, pets, things you like to do. "From Monday through Thursday," says Uehling, "they write about things that are 'true'—that's my condition. It's important to me that they learn to appreciate that their lives are worth writing about. On Fridays, however, we write about anything we like, and here the children can fantasize, which some of them love to do."

That Uehling is so concerned with the children's self-appreciation stems from their alienation within the school and, to some extent, in the society outside the school as well. These children have been judged to be "learning disabled," a label that defines no specific thing, but that means a distinct inability to "keep up" with children of the same age in reading, writing, physical activity, or other standard facets of school life. Understandably, these children often find it difficult to work with their peers and may be either severely withdrawn or unusually disruptive.

43

In Fairfax County, Virginia, where Elly Uehling teaches, some of the most severely affected children are taken out of their regular classes and brought together in special classes, like Uehling's, where they learn all the subjects except music and physical education. The class size is small, because it is felt that these children will benefit most from much individual attention, and because the step is not taken lightly. A long process of screening for sensory-motor difficulties is undertaken before placing a child in this class, since every effort is made to keep the child "mainstreamed" in a regular school classroom. Thus, Uehling's class of seven is comprised of third, fourth, and fifth graders from four different schools.

The classroom, which appears so normal—except for the small class size—is fraught with paradox, as Uehling sees it. While her goal is to bring these children up to the learning level of other nine and ten year olds so that they can again be mainstreamed, she sees this result as highly unlikely, except in one or two cases. She worries not only that the children's disabilities will keep them from making rapid progress, even with special attention, but also that the "specialness" of the class will make them even less able to readjust to the social environment of the typical classroom. So she has tried to balance her curriculum between independent deskwork (math exercises and the like) and one-to-one or one-to-two sessions that focus on particular deficiencies of the students. She knows that these children need to develop self-reliance, hence self-confidence, and that these qualities will lead to their ability to work productively in a larger, more heterogeneous group.

So, on this October morning, as on most mornings, when the children have completed their journal entries, the group subdivides into pairs or individuals who go about distinct tasks: while Sheba, Tyron, and Molly are doing assigned reading or arithmetic at their desks, Uehling talks with Daniel and Fred about their journal entries, teacher aide Howe helps Jason with his spelling, and Mark takes his turn at the computer at the back of the room. The roles will change throughout the morning, as Uehling and Howe give their attention to each child, while the others work by themselves. The atmosphere is cheerful and businesslike. The children seem secure in the knowledge that they'll get whatever help they need.

How does the way language is used in this classroom contribute to this atmosphere? One vital manifestation of Uehling's use of language as a learning tool is the daily journal. As the very first assignment of the day, the journals demand the children's attention and their independence. The journal is a group activity, yet it encourages the children to create, to pursue some of their own ideas. On any given day the children will work in their journals about twenty minutes. Just as their independence in choosing topics is sacrosanct, so is what they say. Each day, in the time she gives to working individually or in pairs with the children, Uehling invites each child to read aloud his or her journal entry and to talk about it. She never corrects their words in these sessions. A misspelling may find its way into a spelling lesson later in the week, but for now Uehling is the active listener who wants to hear of the child's latest adventure or project and to find out more through questions. These questions are purposeful: first, they show appreciation for and attention to what the child has written; second, they push the child to reflect further on the events of the story and, over time, to develop a richer feeling for what the reader might like to know from a writer; third, they show the child that a piece of writing is not a static object, but part of a conversation. As such, it may lead to responses, questions, further writings, and so on.

For part of this morning, Uehling talks with Fred about his latest entry, in which the boy describes a weekend Cub Scout visit to the public library, where he was accidentally left behind by the others. Fred has written four cramped lines, perhaps twenty-five words, on his topic—writing comes less easily for him than for any other child in the class. Still, Uehling responds to Fred's very brief story as to a synopsis of any good adventure. Her questions urge Fred to fill in the details and the sequence: why the scouts went to the library, what he read about while he was there, how he got left behind, what he did when he discovered the others had gone, and how he got home. Each question comes easily and naturally during the conversation. Fred warms to the task, his answers becoming more graphic as he realizes that, yes, this *is* a good story. When the interview closes, he tells his teacher that he'll write more about his adventure in his journal and will read it to the class on Friday.

On Friday, Fred will have the chance to reach the wider audience of the class, because on that day Uehling devotes a substantial part of the morning to using the class as a "reading/writing group." In the group, each child reads aloud one of the week's journal entries and the others comment. Because the one-to-one interviews give the children continuous modeling of how comments and questions can help a writer, the children have become good aids to one another in the Friday sessions. "When we first started," Uehling says, "I gave them some direction as to what to talk about." These were basically the same simple guidelines Uehling herself followed in the reading/writing group of which she had been a part in the Northern Virginia Writing Project summer institute, and the guidelines seemed adaptable to her classes because they could be geared to any level of proficiency either of writing or of responding to it. "The children learned very quickly," Uehling says. "They now handle the sessions themselves."

In the reading/writing group, the children play the same role that Uehling plays in the interviews: they are interested listeners who want to tell the writer what they particularly like in the shared entry and what they'd like to know more about. The listeners are also encouraged to talk about incidents in their own lives that are recalled by the writer's entry, though Uehling is careful to keep the conversation from leaping too far from what the writer has brought to the group.

This technique has succeeded so well that the children have asked Uehling for more reading/writing group sessions. This request has posed a dilemma for her. Should she follow this "learning lead" that they have given her, or should she resist it, on the grounds that the children need all the time they currently spend on math, science, reading, computers, etc.—work that Uehling herself considers more "academic," i.e., closer to what the county's Program of Studies has mandated for "regular" fourth and fifth graders? The dilemma is real. The choice seems to lie between increasing and reinforcing the vital, multifaceted learning brought about by the journals and the response groups, and risking, in other subject areas, further separation of her students from those in the mainstream. A possible solution—though questions of time in the classroom are rarely solvable—may be for Uehling to adapt to her teaching of other required subjects the language-rich approach that has worked so well for her with the "personal events" journals and the reading/writing groups. This might mean in science, for example, two or three entries per week in a "science notebook," where students could write how they did in their experiments with sugar crystals and the like, what changes they observed, what problems they faced, what questions they have. If time did not allow every child to share in group discussion one of his or her entries per week, at least some could, and everyone would have the challenge and privilege of helping another student solve a scientific question. Moreover, the children could share their notebooks in pairs or in threes, so that each could get frequent comments on his or her work. The group example set by the Friday sessions would teach the children how to respond to the science entries.

The dilemma Uehling faces is actually a happy one, since it has been occasioned by the success of the journals and the many language activities surrounding them. Whether she extends these techniques to other areas of the curriculum or not, she is seeing that this particular blend of writing, reading, speaking, and listening has helped the children learn. This new expertise would be useful in any class, labeled or not. The children are finding it easier to express themselves both in their writing and their speaking; they are becoming better able to manage their own communication, and that of others, in the whole group. The process also helps them become adept with audiences of different size and composition, since they are learning to write for themselves, their teachers, and their peers; the interviews and the groups teach them how to conduct both dialogues and formal conversations.

Perhaps, above all, the journal keeping, the reading aloud, and the sharing of other people's feelings and experiences are teaching them something vital about the relationship of the self and the world. Elly Uehling said that one purpose of the journals was to help these children appreciate their lives. What the journals also do, because they are in words, is to help the children appreciate *what they say* about their lives. If we accept the theory that we cannot learn anything until we can put it into our own words, then surely we cannot learn anything unless we respect the tools—of which language is one—that we use to make that learning happen. Journals and the process by which they are shared and responded to may not be the only way to bring about this respect, but they have proven to be a powerful one for Uehling's students.

Elly Uehling Comments on Her Teaching:
"I Am Displeased and Very Mad with Mrs. Uehling"

> May 1985
>
> Last night was very bad.
> This morning I am not talking to Mrs. Ueling. . . .
> It is all Because Mrs. Uehling called my mother on the phone
> and said I was not doing my homework. . . .
> I am displeased and very mad with Mrs. Uehling.
> I wish I was in a another class
> I am very sad.
> I wonder why Mrs. Uehling is doing this to me.

Daniel handed this journal entry in as he left for a work period in the library across the hall. The first twenty minutes of the day had been unusually quiet because Daniel, a fifth grader, spent that time giving me very angry looks and not talking to anyone. It was obvious that something was wrong, which he revealed in his full-page journal entry.

I responded in a letter beginning "I am sorry you were so unhappy." I finished the letter just as Daniel came back to get some colored pencils. I had him read it right then. He stuck out a hand and we shook hands. We talked briefly. However, as he left, he said over his shoulder, "But I'm still mad at you!"

That was okay. We had communicated and understood each other a little better, and writing had been the vehicle. I was excited that Daniel had realized that writing, through his journal, was a flexible tool he could use. It was a way by which he could sort out and share his feelings.

When I taught regular classes of third graders, I learned about the children through their journals and saw how the journals helped them build fluency. So when I returned to a Learning-Disabled Self-Contained class after eight years, I naturally tried using journals with my new class to see what would happen. I hoped that journal writing would increase the children's fluency, but I was not even sure they could or would write.

My beginning instructions were: "You may write about anything you want, but if you have trouble thinking of a topic, you may write about how school is going for you." The children wrote, but I found some were writing only one sentence. Here are two of Fred's early entries:

> I wish I could be like superman more power fur. 9-5-85

> I like school because you have lunch. 9-7-85

In my own growth as a writer, I knew that the acceptance and acknowledgment of my reading/writing group was essential to my development of fluency. I tried to build the same atmosphere of acceptance and acknowledgment for the children.

Also, I knew that reluctant third-grade writers needed goals to increase fluency. I started requiring a minimum of three sentences and increasing the minimum number by one each marking period. Often children think that they cannot write, and so they do not. But my students accepted the increases. In fact, when May began, Fred matter-of-factly said, "I guess today we have to write seven." The other children corrected him quickly. We had not started a new marking period, only a new month.

The children occasionally wrote more when a topic gripped them, as Daniel had. Jason, early in the year, wrote about his concerns of fitting into his new class and wrote that he, a fifth grader, was paired up to help a third grader. He was bothered that the third grader could write better than he. Several others wrote about their excitement at having a new boy join our class and their anger at the resulting turmoil of adjustment. Sheba wrote about her pleasure at being chosen for the sub-patrol and her devastation at being labeled "LD."

This year has been a year of searching for the connection between writing and learning with my class of learning-disabled students. Most of them were labeled distractable, but their problem could also be called undisciplined thinking. They had a hard time focusing on a task, for whatever reason, and would rather flow with any distraction, whether internal or external. I felt that writing would help them focus their thinking. It did not matter that the writing might be unreadable later. Few rules existed, so the journal was a safe place where they could gain confidence by putting thoughts into words on paper. The journals, therefore, were a logical starting point.

As the year of "what happens if" progressed, the children wrote stories and had reading/writing groups almost every Friday. We published class books and individual ones. They developed a strong sense of ownership, authority, and voice in their writings. This sense of individuality became particularly obvious one Friday when Sheba did not want to share her story with the reading/writing group. An aide, working with the school publishing center, had spent some time helping Sheba with her story. But apparently the aide, in her desire to help, had helped too much. Through tears, Sheba exclaimed, "She may be right and the story may be better, but it's not what I want!" The empathy for her from the others touched me greatly. Sheba asked me to rewrite her story just as she wanted it. As I remember, we disbanded the reading/writing group right then, each child returning to his or her work, and I acted as a scribe for Sheba. Many others had this sense of ownership, which Daniel expressed well on another Friday in a reading/writing group. The children were offering Daniel ideas. His reply to them was "Yes, but it's *my* paper!" We all were quiet, accepting his declaration, and I felt very proud of my class.

Through writing the children have often discovered, as did Daniel, what they think and feel. I have also used writing to help them define and clarify their thoughts in the more cognitive areas. In science, for example, a unit on rocks required that characteristics or qualities of the rocks be defined. In order to organize their observations, the children were to write on a chart what they found out about each rock: color, weight, texture, hardness, flakiness. As we discussed the rocks, I recorded our mutual adjectives and adverbs on the board.

"How would you describe rock number three?" I asked.

"Black."

"It's shiny."

"That's a good word." I wrote *shiny* on the blackboard.

"It's got smooth parts."

"But it's got sharp points."

There were many "black" rocks that needed to be classified further: shiny, glassy, flaky, smooth, smoky. We talked about subtle differences in meaning, such as *glassy* versus *shiny*. Many of the children entered into the discussion, but they resisted committing their language to paper. It was the Oh-you-mean-I-have-to-write-it-down? reflex. When they knew that they had to record the information, they looked at the rocks more closely. Thus, language became a tool to clarify their observations through the act of labeling the characteristics of rocks.

In another science unit on caterpillars and butterflies, I used more writing. I asked the children to observe, talk about, draw, and write about their observations. I found the first set of papers discouraging. Some students hardly wrote anything about what they saw. But, I reminded myself, I was asking them to do some tasks that they resist—visually absorbing information, translating those ideas into words, and then putting those words on paper. Many of the children in my class had a hard time processing information and focusing visually in their daily lives, so it was understandably difficult for them to deal with a new experience: creepy, crawly, one-inch-long caterpillars. I was asking them to "look and write"—to discipline their observations and thinking and to translate them into the act of writing those thoughts on paper. I persisted, and, happily, the children have shown improvement in being able to write down more of what they see.

Tyron's first writing about the caterpillars was brief and vague:

> Today is April 1985 First day. Mess. uehling brought some cater-
> pillars are neat.

This says very little about what he was observing. On the second day, Tyron began to record what he saw:

> Some caterpillars are trying to Form a net. The caterpillars are
> trying to form into a chrysalis. one looks like he is brek Dancing

On the third day, Tyron was more detailed:

> on his back he has bristles. And he moves with his muscles of his
> body. And sometimes he just sites on my paper. He trys to spin a
> weeb on my arm. But they are neat. And I wish I could have him
> for a pet.

Fred showed similar progress. He began by writing:

> A caterpillar has 19 legs. We have six larva.

A few days later, he wrote:

> One of the chysails hatch and a butterfly was come out it had
> grump up wings. A butterfly can tocket to a other butterfly. A
> butterfly wing has two hours in to his wings to dry. There are

only one caterpillar left. One of the butterfly are having a hurt wing.

During these days of looking at, talking about, drawing, and writing about the caterpillars, I gave my students information and encouraged them to use descriptive words. We shared interesting phrases from their writings or comments, and I praised their fluency. I tried to establish an atmosphere of involvement in the miracle of life before us. I felt pleased that their ability to generate ideas had improved.

These examples show the children's progress, even within a brief time span of a few days. Most of the children progressed in a similar way. I feel progress was made because they understood what was expected and because a written product was required.

Two passages from Donald Murray's *Write to Learn* (1984) sum up my present attitude toward language and learning:

> Writing, in fact, is the most disciplined form of thinking. It allows us to be precise, to stand back and examine what we have thought, to see what our words really mean, to see if they stand up to our own critical eye, make sense, will be understood by someone else. (4)

> Words are the symbols for specific information. We use words so that we can arrange information into meaningful patterns. Words are a sort of shorthand by which we can capture, comprehend, and communicate experience. Man is the animal that uses words to think and share. (17)

The children in my class have begun to realize that they, too, have power to communicate their ideas—their fears, fantasies, and frustrations—through their writing.

Reference

Murray, Donald. *Write to Learn*. New York: Holt, Rinehart and Winston, 1984.

6 "If I Saw the President, He'd Probably Call My Mom": The Many Uses of Language in the Speech Therapy Class

I am not comfortable here. As a teacher of writing, I have seen in student after student the success of my patience in allowing fluency and technical competence to grow with no need for my hyper-attentiveness to matters of correctness. As one who talks with teachers at all levels, I feel time and time again their joy as they relate the results of trusting to the "process," as it has been described by Emig, Britton, and others. In the language-rich classes I have studied, from first grade through college, I have seen children and adults writing and conversing easily and happily, excited about their learning and proud of themselves and each other.

The younger children and most of the older ones, too, are by no means polished writers. All are learning, growing gradually day by day, often imperceptibly, often dramatically. Their speaking, too, improves step by almost unnoticeable step. I know this and I trust in it; consequently, I do not, and would not, interrupt my attention to my five-year-old son Christopher's excited explanation of the workings of a gasoline engine to ponder his frequent replacement of *th* by *d* or *s*. I fear that I would violate his sense of order and do some small but definite damage to his integrity were I to call attention to the sound rather than the sense of what he says. I might even make him afraid to speak. Hence, I try not to worry about imperfections that, I trust, will pass with time and talk.

That is why I am uncomfortable here, in this, a speech therapy class. I voice my concern to Cynthia Dietz, the speech resource teacher at Orange Hunt Elementary School, who will work today with some ten small groups of children ranging in age from six to twelve; their identified speech problems include speech anxiety, stuttering, and unsatisfactory pronunciation of various sounds. From her words, it is clear that Dietz has carefully considered this issue many times before; indeed, she confronts it every time she must decide whether a particular child, whom the child's teacher has brought to her attention, really needs the two to three special periods per week in the therapy class.

"We know," she says, "that many children in kindergarten and first grade still can't pronounce some common sounds. One of my priorities is to help the classroom teacher recognize the difference between normal development and the problem—relatively rare—that needs attention." Almost as important as the speech therapy program, Dietz says, is the assurance she can give the primary teacher that he or she need not concern himself or herself, nor the children, with most pronunciation difficulties.

Dietz goes on to say, however, that on occasion a teacher will not perceive a more serious speech problem because the teacher is doing what he or she is supposed to do; namely, the teacher is paying close attention to *what* a child is saying rather than how it sounds. In these cases, Dietz's diagnostic expertise is especially valuable. One way by which she determines whether or not to recommend a student to the program is to observe how his or her difficulty affects the student's social relations and classroom performance. If the effect is insignificant, then she won't risk perhaps creating an identity problem for the child by adding the stigma of placement in the program. She will recommend speech therapy when the difficulty seems clearly to be inhibiting communication, learning, and the building of friendships.

The problems of diagnosis are relatively straightforward when a child of seven or older seems to have continuing difficulty pronouncing certain common sounds, with the difficulty great enough to limit the teacher's ability to understand the child. The child will simply be enrolled in Dietz's speech therapy center for as long as deemed necessary and helpful. Limiting diagnosis to a "speech" problem becomes more difficult when the symptom is stuttering or extreme reticence. In many cases, the symptom is stress-related, and a major function of the therapy is to help both teacher and student determine the conditions that are most likely to produce the speech difficulty, as well as the means that may help relieve the anxiety causing it. Thus, what goes on in the program varies markedly with the problems of the children. The children in each group tend to have similar problems and to be fairly close in age.

Though Dietz attends closely to the children's pronunciation or to other formal problems, my discomfort over this focus on correctness dissolves as I watch how she works. All the sessions in her class involve much talk between teacher and student and among the students themselves. What this class shares with the others I have observed for this study is respect for the power of language, if used in all its modes and for many tasks, to create a humane environment that prizes people and their working together. The curriculum here is narrower than in the elementary classrooms of the other teachers, and so is the scope of time (thirty minutes per group per day), yet Dietz's center seems no less language intensive.

With those groups of children having difficulty pronouncing certain sounds, much of the work aims directly at the problems and consists primarily of exercises in pronunciation. For example, Dietz will ask the children to read words off cards, to name pictured objects, or to read riddles or silly stories. There will always be a creative element to such exercises; e.g., the children will have to think up a sentence for the single words they read or the objects they name. This not only makes the exercises more interesting; it also gives Dietz a chance to listen for pronunciation in context.

Sometimes she kindles small competitions within groups, as when she reads a word and then asks the children to think of opposite terms. Since the different connotations of a word may make for several viable "opposites," such games invariably lead to further discussion.

Another dimension of the language interaction gives the children responsibility for teaching one another. Although the groups Dietz teaches are small—no more than six in a period—she gives pairs of students separate tasks in order to vary the types of interaction and the learning challenges. For example, one member of a pair will read aloud (in a moderate tone) to the other, who has been instructed to count his or her partner's correct productions of key sounds. Dietz does not intend to get an accurate evaluation from this exercise; like the self-evaluation of the daily research in Carin Hauser's class, this assignment gives the students another conscious perspective on their work. To evaluate their partners, the students have to *listen* to the sounds spoken and *compare* the heard pronunciation to their own ideas of what is correct. Hence, the listeners themselves "practice" the sounds, even if not vocally.

In the past two years, since participating in the Northern Virginia Writing Project summer institute, writing, too, has become an essential part of Dietz's speech curriculum. With the children having difficulty with certain sounds, this addition means, for example, a homework assignment in which each child writes the physical directions for going from the speech therapy center to another place in the school. The children read their directions aloud to the group during the next session and ask the others to guess the place to which they have traveled. Dietz asks the children to practice their readings at home beforehand, "using your best sounds." Again, she is using the game potential of the small group to focus both speaker and listener closely on the words, since each word will be important toward guessing the secret place. Dietz also knows that the act of composition, plus the expectation of performance, will keep the children more attuned to words than any prewritten exercise can. Besides, the directions game is more fun.

The speech therapy center is a small room containing a table surrounded by six chairs; this forms the setting for informal, yet purposeful, discussion. When children who stutter or who are otherwise inhibited speakers enter the center, both the *how* and the *why* of language change for Cynthia Dietz. Language activities for these children are intended to put them at ease, so that they can confront directly the fact of their difficulty and consider how they might overcome it. It should not surprise the visitor that the children do not keep silent and that they stutter less frequently in the center. As both Dietz and the children themselves will tell you, they stutter most severely when they are frightened, as in the presence of an adult whose acceptance of them is uncertain. As one eight-year-old boy told me, "I only stutter when I see a supreme commander. If I saw the president, he'd probably call my mom." The children know that Dietz will not criticize their speech—nor what they say—and so they talk freely.

Writing plays an important part in this liberating process. Like Elly Uehling, Dietz has been experimenting this year with regular, in-class journal writing, which the students read to others in their group. What the students write about varies from day to day. Before they write, Dietz and the children spend a minute or two saying what they might write about and getting the tacit approval of the others. One child's idea might become the common theme for everyone's writing. At other times, Dietz will suggest that the children write something about their talking or about how they feel when they must talk in certain situations. For the younger children (some are as young as six), these sessions will sometimes produce no more than a brief sentence in the five to ten minutes allotted for writing. Volume is not important to Dietz. What is important is that the children come to see writing as another friendly method of expression, indeed a way of expressing themselves when the spoken word becomes difficult. Relying on the inherent power of written composing to generate ideas for the writer, she also sees this language mode as potentially helping her students feel prepared for perhaps frightening occasions on which they may be called on to speak. To ensure that the writing itself will not become a source of fear for the children, she makes every effort to show acceptance of what they write. When, for example, a six-year-old girl says that she doesn't know how to spell a certain word, Dietz asks her how she spelled it and praises her for the correctly phonetic, though technically incorrect, spelling she gives. When one of the other children gives her the correct spelling, both children have reason to feel good about their contributions.

With something tangible—their journal entries—to share with the others, every child can feel proud of his or her contribution to the discussion. Since the entries are brief, all students have the opportunity to contribute within the short period. Dietz's comments on these writings are frequently questions that probe the connection between the writing and the expressed focus of the group, i.e., the speech difficulty. When one boy reads, for instance, "If I killed a dog, I'd be scared to tell the owner," Dietz refrains from commenting on the obvious violence; instead, she seeks the reason for the child's fear: "Why do you think you'd be scared? Is it because you'd killed the dog, or because you'd be afraid of stuttering?" While the boy considers his answer, another child says—and stutters as he does so, for the only time in the period—"It's hard to talk to someone when you know they're mad at you." The first boy nods in agreement. The writing has given the writer the chance, and the tool, to express a feeling that he might have had a hard time saying aloud. It has given the other boy an insight, plus the courage to speak his own fear, even though it is clearly difficult for him to do so. From the exchange, Dietz learns something about both boys, knowledge that she can build on in later sessions.

Needless to say, reacting and responding to entries such as this requires a good deal of forbearance. The children trust Dietz with words and feelings that they may not feel comfortable sharing with anyone else, including—sometimes especially—their parents. Because Dietz is a speech specialist, she works to restrict her observations and conclusions to those with direct bearing on the problems she is addressing, even though those problems may have psychological causes that are outside the limits of her expertise. Hers is not a comfortable position. It would be perhaps easier for her to conduct more predictable, less interactive sessions for these students, giving them few or no opportunities to express themselves; however, without the writing and the open discussion, she could not become aware of the differences among her students, differences crucial to her treatment of their stuttering or their fear of speaking. Moreover, by making the center a language-rich environment, she gives the children an opportunity to succeed in speech, to make writing a friend rather than an enemy, and to begin to overcome their reticence by talking about events and feelings that had formerly daunted them. Yes, it is disconcerting and even frightening to have one's speech problems—the tangible signs of one's fear—probed by a teacher and by one's fellow classmates. But when the scrutiny takes place in a classroom like that of Cynthia Dietz, where language is always a way to freedom and good feeling, not to further shame, then fear gives way to comfort. For some of the children, the speech program may be their first comfortable place, and if it is the first, it may be the first of many.

Cynthia Dietz Comments on Her Teaching: "It's Square and Has Lots of Paper in It"

"To . . . To . . . Tony is absent and Joey is ta . . . ta . . . taking a test today, Mrs. Dietz," announced Steven as he stood in the door of the small speech room.

"I guess it's you and I then, Steven. That will be a nice change—just the two of us."

"What do . . . do . . . do you want to do?" he asked, moving the few feet to a stand beside my desk, where I was seated.

"Hmmmm . . . ," I thought aloud. "Good question. What shall we do?"

"We . . . We . . . We could write in our journals. Mine's in my speech fo . . . folder," suggested the lanky eight year old, his straight brown hair falling into his eyes.

"Great idea! Mine's right here."

We each found a blue primary chair and gathered around the child-sized table in the center of the room. Ignoring the bookshelf, mirror, and mobile, we nestled comfortably amidst the surrounding walls of word lists and brightly colored action posters.

"What shall we write about today?" I asked.

"Well, we . . . we . . . we could write . . . write about our ne . . . nervous habits. You know, the stuff we just do, like blink your eyes. Stuff . . . Stuff like that."

"Good idea, Steven. I have one and I need to write about it. Let's think about what we do and why we do it."

We wrote steadily and quietly for about ten minutes.

"That felt good, Steven. Can I share first today? Would that be all right?"

"Sure, go ahead," he replied, blinking his eyes with deliberate movements as he spoke.

I read aloud my entry about biting my fingernails and rubbing my fingers together. I told Steven when and why I do these things, how doing them never makes me feel any better, and how hard it is for me to stop.

"Hey, you do that, too? So do I! The thing with your fingers, I mean. I do it sometimes, too," Steven blurted out with obvious surprise. "Can I read mine now?"

"Yes. Please do. I'd like to hear it."

Steven read what he had written:

3-15-85

> One of my neverse habtais is in my anlke I move a bone up and down I don't know why I do it another habit is taping my fingrs I think I do that because I haave waited for a long time like a friend coming from Newyork another habit is shaking my head I do not know why I do that.

I was particularly interested in Steven's head shaking and finger tapping. I had noticed these habits earlier and was concerned that they were becoming secondary characteristics of his stuttering. If these activities were related, if they were a part of his stuttering pattern, then his therapy would need to address the issue and deal with their elimination.

From the ensuing discussion, I learned that Steven made no connection between the gestures and his speech. Although he tapped his fingers only when he was impatient and admitted to shaking his head "almost all the time," he was not consciously using either activity to aid his talking.

As Steven left my room and headed back to his class, I felt pleased that he had willingly written—and talked—about his nervous habits, and I was relieved that he did not relate them to his talking. I was not overly concerned that he did not complete any articulation drill, nor was I worried that he did not practice fluency exercises. There would be other classes for that.

I valued the session because our writing and talking made Steven aware of himself and his idiosyncrasies. He learned that his habits, like his stuttering, were things that he did rather than things that happened to him; things that he controlled rather than things that controlled his being.

Children who stutter often are confused about their speech patterns. They cling to erroneous beliefs about why they have trouble talking and make mistaken assumptions about what helps them to talk better. Vague and misleading, these beliefs can interfere with the child's progression toward fluency.

Most young stutterers view their blocks as events that happen to them rather than as behaviors they exhibit. Accepting the responsibility for the way one speaks is often an important—and sometimes difficult—step in therapy. After accepting their speech as a behavior that they exhibit, these children acknowledge it as something they can change.

One Monday morning, I gave Steven, Tony, and Joey a report portfolio filled with twenty-five pages of third-grade tablet paper. My introduction and instructions were concise:

> These are your journals. We will write in them at the beginning of class every Monday and Friday. You may write any other time you wish. Most of the time each of you may write about whatever you want. Sometimes we will suggest ideas for all of us to write about. We will write for five to ten minutes, and then share our writing.

Steven and his classmates exhibited speech disorders of both articulation and fluency, and at times evidenced accompanying emotional difficulties. These boys were reluctant to talk about their speech, but I hoped they would be willing to write about it. Through directed freewritings I wanted them to explore their talking and their thoughts about it. I believed that writing and sharing the journals would give expression to feelings and concerns about talking.

I accepted anything from the boys and respected everything they wrote and shared. Most of the time I would verbally acknowledge their efforts and thank them for sharing their thoughts. Occasionally I would make a written comment in the journal to verify a perception or to ask for additional information.

Our discussions after sharing the written entries often became directly related to their speech, even if their entry topics were not. We heard about hard-fought soccer games, exciting trips to the zoo, fun-filled bar mitzvahs, and overt sibling rivalries. We learned about being a young stutterer and what it felt like to try to talk to different people in various situations.

The journals were accepted by two of the boys from the start. On the first day, seven-year-old Joey wrote:

> I like my journal. It is neat. I can write in it. There is lots of paper.

Steven's first entry read:

> I am very, happy about keeping a journal it is fun keeping a journal I have never had a journal before it is square and has lots of paper in it it is neat to have a journal.

Tony was more reluctant to write than the others, and often failed to bring his speech folder or his journal to class. When given paper and asked to write with us, Tony found pencils to sharpen, books to read, and pictures to examine. As the weeks went by and we shared our writings regularly, Tony gradually became more willing to write. Although he readily participated in the discussions following a journal reading, Tony remained the most reluctant to read his own entries.

Our journal writing was not always easy, and not always fun. One day I said, "Today let's write anything about our talking," thinking that the openness of my request would make it less threatening and more acceptable to the boys. My suggestion was met with moans and complaints.

"I don't like to do that," said Steven.

"Me neither," added Joey.

"Do we have to?" pleaded Tony.

"Well, I guess not," I said, adjusting my request to their reactions. "But I really am interested in why you don't like to write about it. Can we write about that?"

The boys willingly wrote their reasons. Joey indicated:

> I don't like to write about my talking because it is very very very inbaresting.

Tony, rather than reading his entry aloud, commented, "I don't want to read mine be . . . be . . . because I'm too embarrassed." Steven's entry echoed Tony's words:

> I don't like to write about my talking because I get enbaressted when I read it because they might laugh.

The boys shared their shame and fear, and when no one laughed, they learned that these feelings could be aired and addressed.

At times, I suggested topics for directed freewritings or asked for suggestions from the boys. They examined their best and worst talking, relating the varying situation, subject, and audience. They described their stuttering in terms of what they did, what they heard, and what they felt. They explained what they liked best about their speech and what they most wanted to change. They wrote about speech class activities and what they learned from these activities. They discovered how they felt about themselves and the way they talked, and the impact these feelings had on their speech. I wrote as the boys did, and shared my writings and my feelings with them.

I didn't know what to expect when I began journal writing with these three students, but I have been pleased with the results. I am not alone in my respect for this activity. When asked to comment on the use of journals in speech class, the most reluctant writer willingly read his entry:

> I think it's good to share our thoughts because it's fun, we found out what each other had to say, sometimes I felt happy, sad, funny, or just the same.

Writing has offered the boys an appropriate outlet for their feelings, and sharing their writings has helped them deal with their fear, shame, and anxiety about their talking. Our discussions worked to clarify the myths about stuttering and encouraged the beliefs that result in normal speech. Using the journal as a basis for discussion has enabled these students to reconsider, if not to change, attitudes, beliefs, and feelings that affect the way they talk.

7 Language, Language Everywhere: Learning in Grade Six

The motto of life is "Give and take." Everyone must be both a giver and a receiver. He who is not both is as a barren tree.

—Hasidic Writings (cited in Al Lengel's packet on the research paper for his sixth-grade students)

Just around the corner from Carin Hauser's third-grade classroom at Louise Archer School in Vienna, Virginia, is Al Lengel's sixth-grade classroom. Children who have been through her language-rich curriculum are not surprised when they enter his. But the adult visitor is slightly overwhelmed, at first glance, by the profusion of verbal riches. Student writing is on display everywhere: science projects, simulation games, collage/autobiographies, poems. On one wall a display titled "Wolf Talk" includes information on the drive to protect wolf species in the United States and typed poems by the children expressing their empathetic reflections on the issue. Another display, "Synchronology" (Lengel's version of the "Student of the Week" exhibit), contains photographs and commentary by Julie, this week's honoree. What makes the display a "synchronology" is Julie's time line of her life, along which she has listed important personal events and the important world and national events occurring during this same time span. Along another wall, Lengel has displayed collage/poems that the children have written and designed about loved ones, the collages containing photographs and illustrations of favorite articles.

I have visited Al Lengel's classroom many times before this December afternoon (my son Jeff was his student two years ago), so I have grown to expect the new ideas, projects, displays. I have also grown to expect the singular ambience of his classroom, appearing unstructured but actually highly organized and complex. For example, many of the students have been occupied this morning in the school auditorium, where they are rehearsing the class production of *A Midsummer Night's Dream*. Plays in Lengel's classes are semiannual events, with sometimes two plays, one Shakespearean and one modern, in production simultaneously. So on this occasion the classroom is fairly empty, except for seven children whom Lengel has gathered to answer my questions about their work. On other times I have visited, the classroom has been a welter of activity, the children at work in small clusters on any number of projects, from designing board games based on the novel *Watership Down* to comparing their opinion essays on current issues. On such occasions, Lengel is an all-purpose consultant, his desk the place to which individuals or groups come as questions or differences of opinion arise. Since the students have been for the most part well prepared for their tasks by Lengel's written instructions and whole-class discussions, the students largely direct themselves, so that Lengel can use much of this time to work with individuals on subjects or concepts with which they are having difficulty.

This complex organization depends on both the students' self-reliance and their mutual respect, as well as on the teacher's trust of his students, which is perhaps the most basic ingredient of Lengel's success. He assumes their ability to work independently and with one another on challenging, often complicated projects. This does not mean that the children don't need guidance. His handouts manifest his careful planning of the interactive steps of each project. But he does assume that his students will be able, after discussion of the handouts, to follow the instructions, ask questions when they get stuck, and work for the mutual good of the group.

Talking and writing are the feedback modes built into the system. Because, as the "Insect Identification" handout shown below exemplifies, Lengel sees student writing frequently, he can troubleshoot for both work teams and individuals. In addition, since the students know that they can ask procedural and content questions at any time and not fear his disapproval, he is not likely to miss a problem in group interaction or in conceptual understanding.

The subjects that he teaches, or, rather, that he wants his students to learn about, also show his respect for them. The students explore knowledge through exploring issues; e.g., endangered species, world population, computerization, environmental pollution, nuclear weapons. From the challenges he gives them and the methods he asks them to employ, students learn that knowledge is not an accumulation of textbook statements (although a textbook may be *one* source of information), but a multifaceted ability to gather data, sift among the pertinent and the unnecessary, compare interpretations, establish one's own point of view, defend that perspective, and change it as one's data grow. In Lengel's class, students' opinions are always respected: with so much emphasis on discussion and group work, it is clear that the students are expected to see one another as perhaps the most important resource of information and ideas. Nevertheless, as illustrated by the following sample handout, "Insect Investigation: A Survey," the exchange of opinions is augmented by handouts, textbook articles, library books, magazines, newspapers, and whatever other sources the students find useful.

Insect Investigation: A Survey

Name _____   Started _____

I. General Discussion
   A. Discuss handouts: "Ten Common Insect Orders," etc. Know important information for quizzes and graded discussions.
   B. Questions to answer (Science spiral)
      1. What is an insect? Name the distinguishing features or body parts.
      2. How is an insect different from other small animals? Choose a small animal and compare it with an insect, pointing out differences in needs, behavior, and characteristics. (Make a table or chart.)
      3. Describe the habitat of any common insect.
      4. What is the importance or value of insects? What are their relationships to plants and people? Do insects contribute anything of value to the planet Earth?
   Due Date: _____

II. Debate Resolution
   Let us debate the following: In light of the expected sudden increase in population (the world population of 4.7 billion people will double by the year 2022), hunger and starvation may become widespread and common in *your* lifetime. In one way or another these problems will affect you. *It is resolved* that insects as a cheap and ready source of protein should be an important and staple part of the American diet, and *it is further resolved* that this trend should be established at an early age: school lunches will include toasted ants, fried grasshoppers, and chocolate-covered crickets. All treats like candy bars and ice cream will be composed of nuts and small, toasted, crunchy insects. School lunches will be purchased by every child in the school.
   A. Decide which side you wish to argue (affirmative or negative).
   B. Informal debate session.
   C. C.P.S. groups and follow-up discussions (graded).

III. Important Science Text Pages to Read
   A. *Life in the Environment*—Unit III, "Living Things," pages 165 to 237.
   B. Be sure to read all pages as there will be quizzes and chapter tests. We will read selections together and discuss important parts.
   C. "Insect of the Future" three-person artwork.

IV. Written and Oral Report
   A. Using materials and books from the school library and the Vienna Public Library, choose an insect *order* which interests you and prepare a general report on this particular order. Emphasize the common characteristics of the insects in this particular order.
   B. In the second part of your report, choose *one* specific example of insect within the order about which you have written and report on

the insect example in detail. This is the main part of your report. Include:

1. Appearance
2. Range
3. Habits and reproduction
4. Metamorphosis type
5. Food
6. Item of interest
7. Illustration(s) labeled
8. Folder, title page, bibliography
9. Minimum of 3 pages
10. Brief oral presentation

C. Finally, make a short one-page report on a spider or arachnid of your choice.

Due Date: _____

It is impossible to conceive of the children's developing this complex, "adult" understanding of knowledge without the rich language interactions Lengel organizes. The interactions—the debate, for example—also ensure that what the students learn will be remembered, because they will have had to use this information and make it their own in order to substantiate the viewpoints they have chosen. Moreover, since the debate is a competitive structure requiring response as well as exposition, the students are called on to listen intently to and to understand the arguments of their opponents in order to contest these arguments.

One reason why competition can succeed in this environment without endangering the community of the class is that there are also many noncompetitive, mutually supportive activities. In addition, the children get frequent practice with a modified debate format that Lengel has named "Opinion/Commentary." This assignment exposes the children to reasonable criticism of their ideas. Each week, Lengel announces an issue in the news as the subject for individual three-paragraph essays. He also gives each student the name of a partner with whom he or she will swap essays, so that each may write a paragraph or two of commentary on the other's work. In the course of a year, each child will have compared points of view and evidence on many issues with most members of the class. Lengel grades both the essays and the commentaries for the completeness and accuracy of the information. He also judges them on tone, having admonished the commentators to be "specific and polite."

In such an environment, it's no wonder that the children can talk easily and knowledgeably to an outsider about how and what they learn. The seven members of the class whom I question on this visit excitedly describe the two research projects they have completed since September. The first, which extended over two months and included some twenty steps, allowed the students to write on any topic, the main stipulation being that they wanted "to learn about [the subject] in great depth," as Lengel wrote in his printed guidelines. The projects took students to many different sources for information and, since this was an extensive assignment, required them to learn principles of organization and record keeping that most children don't encounter until high school. With a logical set of subtasks and frequent submissions, Lengel could keep the students on schedule and measure their progress. In keeping with his emphasis on interaction, this progress depended on a good deal of feedback from others, including fellow students and parents.

The topics of the children with whom I speak show great variety, evidence of Lengel's encouragement of individuality. The students name Pompeii, Thomas Jefferson, the elements of the periodic table, long-distance running, the moose, tigers, and the effect of diet on the risk of heart attack as their subjects—writing that truly spans the curriculum. Since the projects were interactive, with the students helping each other generate questions to investigate, commenting on rough drafts, and proofreading final copies, the writing process meant hearing about and discussing many topics in many fields other than that which each had chosen. The process and the results of such a project seem not unlike those enacted and achieved by Mary Schulman's first graders, though at an appropriately higher level of sophistication.

The children speak without puzzlement and with great enthusiasm about the effects of this method. Kim comments, "When we talk about our projects, we give each other new ideas." Charles continues, "When I hear someone else's ideas, I suddenly understand some ideas that have been floating around in my own brain."

The second projects that the students discuss were more restricted in focus, but demanded a variation in approach that would tap still other creative resources. In Part I of the project, each child was to choose a different animal on the threatened or endangered species lists. Maria, for example, chose the emperor penguin; Ashley chose the sea otter. The students, with help from their classmates, generated short lists of questions, and then they reported the answers to the class. Part II of the project called on each student to imagine a mythical creature that had developed characteristics that would *prevent* its extinction. The children described and pictured these creatures, explained the threats to their existence, and described the crucial adaptations. As works of fantasy, these projects exercised the students' ability to hypothesize natural or technological solutions to environmental problems, solutions that would require the students to understand the problems. The children speak with obvious pride about their fantastic creatures, on which they had lavished intriguing names: Will's Dimension Beast, Julie's Sir Nicholas, Kim's Fairy-in-a-Flower, Charles's Cifus, and Ashley's Tricker.

This project exemplifies the mingling of the imaginative and the observed, of the reflective and the recorded, that occurs in so much of the work of Lengel's students. The children are respected for their opinions and for their ability to find and express information; they are also respected for their creativity and for their feelings. Poems about wolves, position papers on insect snacks, hypotheses of "Dimension Beasts"—each implies learning that is part of the child, because he or she has exercised the full range of mind—cognitive, analytical, and emotional. When one considers the further dimension added to this growth by the linguistic, social, and emotional challenges of play performance, then the application of language across the curriculum can truly be called comprehensive.

What do the students say about this approach to teaching? Reflecting back on his sixth-grade experience, Jeff analyzed what this comprehensive language-across-the-curriculum approach meant to him:

> Mr. Lengel didn't constantly assign worksheets and sections of the textbook, as most teachers do. He was very creative in presenting information. He made games that were tools to learn, but games that were constructed in such a way that they were very enjoyable to play—not school exercises that were merely called games.
>
> But, even more important, Mr. Lengel gave us freedom. He gave us the sense that we had some power to help ourselves learn and to have what amounted to a good time. He made us feel very free to ask help in anything and free to express our individuality.
>
> Surprisingly, only on very rare occasions did anyone abuse these privileges. The reason for this, I think, is that the kids didn't feel boxed in and so didn't need to "break loose" by doing something reckless.
>
> The freedom he gave us made us feel more confident and sure of ourselves. I can't remember one time that year that I didn't want to go to school.

Al Lengel Comments on His Teaching: Relying on a Thematic Approach

I've been asked to describe how I manage to provide a creative classroom within the confines imposed by our Program of Studies, a comprehensive county program containing a fully articulated set of goals and objectives for each subject area in all grades, K–12. Actually, I've never felt confined by the so-called "restrictions" of this program. In fact, for me, the program provides a sufficiently reliable structure to which the muscle of a language-dominated program adheres. The strategies and techniques could hardly flex without the framework.

Essentially, however, I don't interpret the program as separating the subjects and objectives into discrete blocks of time. I never consider blocks of time as appropriate to teaching a subject. All the areas are language-directed and require an expansion or differentiation within them. Can social studies be separated from reading, speech, and writing? Rather, they are all woven with an obligation to sense, application, and concept building—never to mere minutes.

I rely, therefore, on a thematic approach. A theme provides the impetus when beginning a unit of study. Most themes endure in variation throughout all my units and intercede like motifs awaiting validity as the child's growing experience and perspective light them anew.

One such theme is *change*. Consider change as a theme, or cog, from which numerous realizations stem. Change has movement and dimension—easily perceived through a ten year old's experience and ability. Within this emphasis on change, my intent is clear: change is continual and inevitable. I hope that this is increasingly obvious or real to the child, whereupon the child can discipline himself or herself to understand change, can deal with it creatively, and can even predict change and its inferences.

A unit centering on flight, for example, explores our early, present, and projected associations with flight and investigates the concept in the natural world as well. Content is treated, knowledge is accumulated, and understanding is broadened because the theme stretches across the curriculum and binds the disciplines. The child grasps the sense of change in its ubiquity. The child observes the influence of change and identifies the elusive indicators that suggest imminent change.

I can develop the theme of change whether the class is discussing the dissolution of the Union and the Civil War, or if we are examining the uses and reporting of statistics in various time periods, or as we follow the awesome disintegration of the character of Macbeth.

Another of my favorite themes is *relationships*. One considers values in the society through the mirror of relationships. This theme is developed during class discussions about characters, plot, and associations in books like *Watership Down* by Richard Adams and *A Separate Peace* by John Knowles.

Fragmentation distorts the school day—chorus, strings, band, and computers merely head the list of interruptions or separations. Therefore, having blocks of time relegated to specific subject areas is an idea wholly impractical. The theme unifies the curriculum.

For example, a class discussion of recent Supreme Court decisions dealing with "search" in the school environment and its implications in regard to the Fourth Amendment to the Constitution becomes a blend of social studies and humanities study, as well as an opportunity to build on the process of writing from its brainstorming stage to the final tract.

Formal debating is another exciting and deeply involving speech extension of a current and relevant topic. Debating as a communication model is a lively facilitator of concept building and language proficiency.

One final note in this brief characterization: it is my belief that children essentially need confirming. Each and every child must be supported and confirmed in the validity of his or her point of view. With the example set, children release their own power to confirm their peers in turn.

Author

Christopher Thaiss is Director of the Plan for Alternative General Education at George Mason University and is Associate Director of the Northern Virginia Writing Project. Active in the development of school and college writing-across-the-curriculum programs since 1978, he coordinates the National Network of Writing-across-the-Curriculum Programs, Elementary-University. He contributed to the U.S. Department of Education Project on Writing and Speaking and currently represents the National Council of Teachers of English on an interdisciplinary task force on critical thinking and testing. Thaiss's publications include *Speaking and Writing, K-12: Classroom Strategies and the New Research* (with Charles Suhor) and *Writing to Learn: Essays and Reflections on Writing across the Curriculum.* His articles and reviews have appeared in such publications as *College Composition and Communication, Shakespeare Quarterly,* and *The Writing Center Journal,* and he has contributed chapters to books on dramatic history, the teaching of writing, and writing across the curriculum.